ATOMIC CULTURE

ATOMIC CULTURE

How
We
Learned
to
Stop
Worrying
and
Love
the Bomb

FALLOUT SHELTER

EDITED BY
Scott C. Zeman and
Michael A. Amundson

UNIVERSITY PRESS OF COLORADO

Published by the University Press of Colorado
5589 Arapahoe Avenue, Suite 206C
Boulder, Colorado 80303

 The University Press of Colorado is a proud member of
the Association of American University Presses.

The University Press of Colorado is a cooperative publishing enterprise supported, in part, by
Adams State College, Colorado State University, Fort Lewis College, Mesa State College, Metro-
politan State College of Denver, University of Colorado, University of Northern Colorado, and
Western State College of Colorado.

The paper used in this publication meets the minimum requirements of the American National
Standard for Information Sciences—Permanence of Paper for Printed Library Materials. ANSI
Z39.48-1992

Library of Congress Cataloging-in-Publication Data

Zeman, Scott C.
  Atomic culture : how we learned to stop worrying and love the bomb / edited by Scott C.
Zeman and Michael A. Amundson.
    p. cm. — (Atomic history and culture series)
  ISBN 0-87081-763-9 (hardcover : alk. paper) — ISBN 0-87081-764-7 (pbk. : alk. paper)
  1. United States—Civilization—1945– 2. Popular culture—United States—History—20th
century. 3. Popular culture—United States—History—21st century. 4. Nuclear weapons—Social
aspects—United States. 5. Nuclear warfare—Social aspects—United States. 6. War and society—
United States. 7. Nuclear energy—Social aspects—United States. I. Amundson, Michael A., 1965–
II. Title. III. Series.
  E169.12Z46 2004
  306'.0973'09045—dc22

                                                                        2004001010

Design by Daniel Pratt

13 12 11 10   10 9 8 7 6 5 4 3

 The publication of this book was made possible in part by a generous grant from the
Nevada Humanities Committee.

Chapter 2 contains a revised version of a chapter from *Inventing Los Alamos: The Creation of Atomic
Culture, 1943–1957* (forthcoming from University of Oklahoma Press), reprinted with the permission of University of Oklahoma Press.

Cover art and chapter opening motif from *Suburban Fallout* by Robert Dohrmann, modified with
permission.

Every reasonable effort has been made to trace the ownership of all copyrighted material in this
book. Any errors that may have occurred are inadvertent and will be corrected in subsequent
editions, provided notification is sent to the publisher.

Contents

Illustrations

Acknowledgments

Several essays in this book were presented at the 1999 "The 50s Turn Fifty" conference at the Western Heritage Center at the University of Wyoming in Laramie and at the 2001 Atomic Culture section of the Southwest Popular Culture Association in Albuquerque, New Mexico. Thanks especially to Peter Rollins for his support and encouragement for the latter. It was in Albuquerque that the idea for this book was born. We give special thanks to Ferenc Szasz for his advice and encouragement from the beginning. Thanks, too, to our students, Scott's 2002 Atomic America class at New Mexico Tech, and Michael's 2002 Atomic Energy and Power class at Northern Arizona University, who read earlier versions of most of the essays in this book and offered their insights and helpful suggestions for revisions.

At the University Press of Colorado, thanks to director Darrin Pratt who supported both this book and the *Atomic History and Culture* series from the start. We also appreciate the strong support of former acquisitions editor Kerry Callahan for getting this going and current editor Sandy Crooms for seeing it through to publication. We appreciate Laura Furney and Daniel Pratt for their great design work and patience. Thanks to Cheryl Carnahan for her great copy editing and everyone else at the press. You all have been wonderful.

We'd also like to thank the history department at Idaho State University who took each of us on as temporary colleagues—in different years—and our own departments at New Mexico Tech and Northern Arizona University for their support.

We are indebted to the Nevada Humanities Council for their grant to subvent Peter Goin's color photographs and to Chuck Rankin at the University of Oklahoma Press for allowing us to use Jon Hunner's work here.

Thanks to Bob Dohrmann for allowing us to use *Suburban Fallout* as the basis for the cover art and chapter headings.

Scott would like to offer special thanks to Chelsea Buffington who endured prolonged discussions of atomic culture, provided many helpful suggestions, and lent her editorial talents to the manuscript, and also to his parents, Dolores and Charles, for their continual support. Michael also thanks his parents, Arlen and Joan, and his sister, Kathy, for their continued support, and friends Steve and Laura—plus Max and Nellie—for listening to him talk about uranium again.

Finally, thanks to all of the contributors to this book, Frank Szasz, Jon Hunner, Peter Goin, Dina Titus, Mick Broderick, and Peter van Wyck, for sharing their talents with us and for their patience. Although we owe all of these people a great deal for their assistance, any errors are own responsibilities.

ATOMIC CULTURE

Introduction

SCOTT C. ZEMAN AND MICHAEL A. AMUNDSON

In his pathbreaking study of early American atomic culture, historian Paul Boyer noted that "if a scholar a thousand years from now had no evidence about what had happened in the United States between 1945 and 1985 except the books produced by the cultural and intellectual historians of that era, he or she would hardly guess that such a thing as nuclear weapons had existed."[1] Since Boyer wrote those words in 1985, a few scholars have followed his lead in filling in this void. For example, Allan M. Winkler's 1993 examination of the "shifting influence" among government officials, scientists, cultural critics, and the public shows how atomic culture became imbedded in American life.[2] Similarly, individual case studies of uranium mining, the Manhattan Project, bomb production, atomic testing, and fallout shelters attest to the growing atomic library.[3] Nevertheless, given the significance of nuclear technology in shaping the past fifty years of American history and culture, much remains to be studied.

The chapters in this volume, which consider a sampling of cultural expressions of atomic energy from the 1940s to the early twenty-first century, begin to close that gap. As Americans came to terms with the reality of atomic energy in the decades after Trinity, Hiroshima, and Nagasaki, their fears, hopes, and concerns found expression not only in governmental debates and media editorials but also in a growing atomic culture.

With the term *atomic culture,* this book examines all types of atomic texts including the traditional "highbrow" (elite) and "lowbrow" (popular) cultural expressions and everything in between including Spiderman comic books, uranium board games, science fiction television shows, mushroom cloud postcards, and atomic-themed motion pictures. It also includes careful analyses of nuclear landscapes past, present, and future including examinations of the Nevada Test Site, the Los Alamos suburbs, and future atomic waste facilities.[4] The major emphasis, however, is on popular culture. Popular culture, as John Fiske has pointed out, is "on the one hand . . . industrialized–its commodities produced and distributed by a profit motivated industry that follows economic interests. But on the other hand, it is of the people, and the people's interests are not those of the industry." Further, Fiske argues, "to be made into popular culture, a commodity must also bear the interests of the people. Popular culture is not consumption, it is culture—the active process of generating and circulating meanings and pleasures within a social system."[5] In other words, popular culture must be just that—popular. Commodities produced by industry, such as records, television, and film, must "bear the interests of the people" for them to become popular culture. The relationship between atomic popular culture and the interests of the industries—and, we should add, the government—is complex, as many of the chapters included here show.

As a relatively new field, atomic cultural history in the United States has not developed its own periodization but has rather followed the basic schema of twentieth-century American history, or the Cold War more specifically. However, this book aims to provide such a structure. Although periodizations are by their very nature artificial constructs, it is hoped that the basic organization developed here will better compare and contrast the historical development of American atomic culture during each period, thus highlighting similar themes as well as differences. The four distinct periods are Early, High, Late, and Post Atomic Culture.

EARLY ATOMIC CULTURE (1945–1948)

The world forever changed on the morning of July 16, 1945, at a site on the Jornada del Muerto in the New Mexican desert. At the moment the flash from seemingly a second sun pierced the sky–precisely at 5:29:45 A.M. Mountain War Time–the engineers, scientists, and servicemen at the Trinity Site liberated the tremendous energy of the atom. The use of atomic bombs against the Japanese cities of Hiroshima and Nagasaki three weeks later officially began the atomic age and with it what we call Early Atomic Culture in the United States. When

Americans first learned of the atomic bombing of Japan, most celebrated, for they believed the end of a long and costly war was close at hand. Like most of the Manhattan Project scientists, the public feeling was euphoric. World War II ended, and revenge had been exacted for Pearl Harbor. The lyrics of a popular country western song, "When the Atom Bomb Fell," recorded in December 1945, attested to this view as it declared the bomb "the answer to our fighting boys' prayers."[6]

Early Atomic Culture first celebrated the bomb and the end of World War II and then taught the American public about cutting-edge science. Both forms shaped public opinion. Examples of the former included an intoxicating beverage known as the "atomic cocktail," a rich dessert spiked with liqueur called the "Atomic Bomb," and an "atomic bomb ring" available through Kix cereal.[7] Comic books provide an interesting example of the latter. When *Dagwood Splits the Atom* hit the newsstands in 1949, it used one of America's favorite characters to teach everyday Americans the basics of atomic theory. After all, if the Bumsteads could understand nuclear physics, so could everyone else. In doing so, Dagwood also informed the American public that atomic weapons were a safe and necessary part of the country's postwar arsenal.

Early Atomic Culture also focused on the potential benefits of the fissioned atom: a vast new source of energy, a potential panacea for disease, perhaps even a world that would forever be free of war—under the protection of an American *Pax atomica*. Early Atomic Culture prospered during the first few years after the end of the war as the United States enjoyed its atomic weapons monopoly. The failure of international atomic control, the start of the Cold War, and the rise of the second Red Scare began to break down this era. The Soviet Union's 1949 explosion of its own atomic bomb in the desert of Kazakhstan brought an important change.

HIGH ATOMIC CULTURE (1949–1963)

The Soviet atomic test—code-named First Lightning—electrified American culture and initiated what can be termed High Atomic Culture. Profoundly shaped by the standoff with the Soviet Union, this period was characterized by a flourishing of atomic culture. High Atomic Culture was fashioned by a variety of events including a uranium boom and bust in the American West, the threat of Soviet nuclear attack, the development of thermonuclear weapons and inter-continental ballistic missiles (ICBMs), the creation of Project Plowshare (to use atomic bombs for engineering purposes), Mutually Assured Destruction, the placement of a continental testing site in Nevada and its subsequent fallout, and the expansion of missile technology.

American culture of the period reflected these concerns and fears. Whether it was Bill Haley and the Comets commenting on the pleasures of a postapocalyptic world in their hit "13 Women" or Roy Rogers protecting national security by chasing down uranium claim jumpers in the film *Bells of Coronado,* popular culture appropriated aspects of the bomb into American culture for entertainment value. Rock and roll songs of the High Atomic era spoke to the residual feeling of hopefulness in often playful, even flippant ways. Skip Stanley's "Satellite Baby" pleaded: "Nuclear baby don't fission out on me ... We're gonna rock it, we're gonna rock it ... Isotope daddy's found out what you are worth"; and the singer of the Five Stars' "Atom Bomb Baby" declared that his dream girl mushroomed him "right up on a cloud."

By attaching one of the most destructive forms of weaponry to such romantic fantasies, High Atomic Culture encouraged Americans to disassociate the devastating potential of nuclear warfare from the realities of everyday life. *The Atomic Kid* (1954) fused uranium mining with atomic testing. In the film, Mickey Rooney is a uranium prospector wandering the Nevada desert where he stumbles into the Nevada Test Site during an atomic blast. Somehow surviving the blast, he spends the rest of the film not only glowing but trying to market himself as the first human to survive an atomic blast. Instead of remembering the real survivors of Hiroshima and Nagasaki, atomic bombs were simply props, with the film's message conveying that exposure to radiation can be fun and profitable.

By the early 1960s the dominant tone of High Atomic Culture began to change. The Cuban Missile Crisis, the Partial Test Ban Treaty, and the assassination of President John F. Kennedy helped trigger a shift in public opinion. The brinkmanship of the Cuban Missile Crisis in particular terrified Americans and the world and highlighted the potential for nuclear catastrophe: the legacy of the hot days of the Cold War and an arms race that had spiraled out of control.

LATE ATOMIC CULTURE:
AMERICAN CULTURE GOES CRITICAL (1964–1991)

By 1964, High Atomic Culture had been replaced by Late Atomic Culture as Americans became more openly critical of nuclear weapons. A major factor in the shifting atomic cultural landscape was the collapse of what historians have called the "Cold War consensus," the general and broad-based support for the government's handling of the Cold War and the concomitant growth and development of America's nuclear stockpile. Domestic and international events dramatically impacted U.S. atomic culture. American involvement in Vietnam, the publication of the Pentagon Papers, and the Watergate scandal furthered questioning of Cold War policies and made many Americans increasingly distrustful of their government. In addition, a growing antinuclear movement and the highly publicized near-disaster at Pennsylvania's Three Mile Island nuclear plant highlighted the dangers associated with nuclear power. Americans also became increasingly aware of the costs to both the people and the landscape from years of underground uranium mining and nuclear testing. During this period atomic culture turned from a focus on selling the bomb to one of exposing its harmful effects.[8]

Writers like Edward Abbey lamented the effects of years of uranium mining on the West's landscape, and Acoma Pueblo poet Simon Ortiz examined its impact on the region's peoples. Journalists and historians began explaining the nation's atomic attractions. Perhaps the best indicator of the changed cultural milieu is seen in Stanley Kubrick's *Dr. Strangelove: Or How I Learned to Stop Worrying and Love the Bomb* (1964). The film's descent into nuclear apocalypse, and its savaging of Cold War ideology and the doctrine of mutually assured destruction, resonated with a culture ready to reevaluate decades of nuclear weapons buildup and one far more critical of what it saw.

The eclipse of Late Atomic Culture coincided with the end of the Cold War. What had been the defining characteristic of the world order changed almost in an instant and left U.S. culture grappling with new ways to understand the significance and meaning of the atom.

POST ATOMIC CULTURE:
NOSTALGIA FOR A BIPOLAR WORLD (1992–PRESENT)

Since the collapse of the Soviet Union and the end of the Cold War, Americans have been living in a Post Atomic Culture. New terms have entered the popular discourse: *loose nukes* and *dirty bombs* have supplanted ICBMs and Mutually Assured Destruction. To be sure, Americans are still concerned with nuclear weapons, especially in the hands of "rogue nations" or terrorists, but the atom seems to have lost its cultural centrality.

Perhaps the most visible example of Post Atomic Culture is the popular television show *The Simpsons*. With its dominating atomic power plant on the horizon, an opening sequence showing Homer accidentally leaving work with a fuel rod, and an entire episode featuring "Blinkie"—a three-eyed fish caught downstream from the plant—the animated saga of America's "Nuclear Family" paints a benign picture of our nuclear past. Even young Bart Simpson's favorite superheroes, "Radioactive Man" and his sidekick "Fallout Boy," wax nostalgic for a positive nuclear past free of investigative reporting.[9]

5

A good barometer of the changing cultural concerns can also be found in the popular superhero Spiderman. Created in 1962 by Stan Lee for Marvel Comics, the original Spiderman gained his superpowers, in true High Atomic fashion, after being bitten by an irradiated spider. In the 2002 big-budget movie version, the spider that imparts Peter Parker with his special powers is genetically altered. Other recent science fiction and fantasy films also reflect a new concern with genetics: the rampaging dinosaurs of *Jurassic Park* (1993) and the genetic profiling of *Gattaca* (1997), for example. The shift from atomic concerns to fears of genetic engineering is telling. Once again, popular culture is serving as a vehicle to express contemporary concerns and issues. The atom no longer expresses current concerns the way it once did. Yet at the same time, the declining concern is also marked by a growing nostalgia for the "good old days" of the Cold War, the bipolar world, and the "security" of the mushroom cloud.

The Post Atomic cultural landscape is a confusing one, and its true direction remains to be seen. The first question is whether the country will even preserve its atomic heritage. As health concerns win out over historic preservation, much of the atomic landscape seems destined for remediation. Other questions concern how the nuclear past will be presented to the American public. The hotly debated 1995 *Enola Gay* exhibit at the Smithsonian was only the first controversy over how our nuclear past will be told. A similar but less publicized incident focused on the selling of earrings shaped like Fat Man and Little Boy—the Hiroshima and Nagasaki bombs—at Albuquerque's National Atomic Museum gift shop. With nuclear tourism taking its first baby steps, future debates are not only certain but will continue to show atomic culture's evolution.[10] A brief examination of this volume's chapters will make for a good starting point.

From *Dagwood Splits the Atom* during Early Atomic Culture to Bart Simpson's thoroughly Post Atomic superhero "Radioactive Man," Ferenc Szasz follows atomic-themed comic books over five decades. His chapter, "Atomic Comics: The Comic Book Industry Confronts the Nuclear Age," shows how comic books first exerted a powerful influence in shaping popular perceptions of the atom before later serving more as a barometer of public opinion.

Los Alamos, New Mexico, resides at the epicenter of U.S. nuclear weapons research, and as Jon Hunner argues in "Reinventing Los Alamos: Code Switching and Suburbia at America's Atomic City," it played a key role in defining the transition from Early Atomic to High Atomic Culture. Begun as a top-secret military research facility during World War II, Los Alamos redefined itself as a postwar suburban community, "code switching" from a wartime military setting to one of single-family homes, public schools, and civil defense drills. In this way, Los Alamos anticipated major trends that came to dominate the social and cultural life of Cold War America.

In "'Uranium on the Cranium': Uranium Mining and Popular Culture," Michael Amundson shows how the U.S. government's need for fissionable materials for its expanding nuclear stockpile in the 1950s triggered a similar boom during High Atomic Culture with everything from board games to movies to rock and roll. After going bust in the 1960s, uranium mining resurfaced during the Late Atomic Period, but this time things were different. Instead of pop culture gimmicks, writers and poets began exposing the more sober problems of long-term health and environmental consequences.

In his chapter, "Confronting the 'Capitalist Bomb': The Neutron Bomb and American Culture," Scott Zeman tracks this same transition from High Atomic to Late Atomic Culture through cultural perceptions of the neutron bomb. Designed to kill people without destroying property, the concept for the neutron bomb first appeared in the late 1950s and was viewed as a futuristic new weapon—an atomic death ray—straight out of science fiction. When the concept resurfaced in the late 1970s, it was no longer viewed as a marvelous new death ray but rather as a morally abhorrent weapon of mass destruction. As Zeman notes, the basic technology behind the device remained the same, but American atomic culture had changed dramatically.

The nuclear past lives within the landscape present. Peter Goin's rephotographs and essay contemplate the remnants of High Atomic Culture on the Post Atomic landscape of today. Through a series of photographs taken of similar subjects more than four decades apart, Goin's images collapse time as they comment on the nuclear landscape then and now. Unlike any other work in this book, his personal comments during the rephotographic experience serve, with the photographs, as new documentary evidence reflecting on how Post Atomic Culture reads the "built environment" of High Atomic Culture.

Another chapter that looks back on five decades of atomic culture is "The Mushroom Cloud as Kitsch" by A. Costandina Titus. The author argues that in the years following the bombing of Hiroshima, the U.S. government consciously deployed images of the mushroom cloud to garner and sustain support for America's nuclear weapons program. Mirroring the broader shift from High to Late Atomic Culture, the year 1963 marked a watershed in cultural perceptions of the mushroom cloud. Just as testing went underground following the Partial Test Ban Treaty, so too did the ubiquitous mushroom cloud fade from public sight. A resurrection of the mushroom cloud as kitsch corresponded to the transition to Post Atomic Culture. In this changed cultural milieu, Titus notes, the mushroom cloud became a nostalgic symbol of a bygone era.

By analyzing an impressive array of post–Cold War nuclear films in his chapter "Is This the Sum of Our Fears? Nuclear Imagery in Post–Cold War Cinema," Mick Broderick provides insight into the dominant themes expressed in Post Atomic films. Broderick finds three important "deviations" in recent motifs: first, a focus on the Kennedy era and the Cuban Missile Crisis; second, an emphasis on the potential liberating force of nuclear weapons; and third, concerns about nuclear weapons in the hands of terrorists. As with Post Atomic mushroom cloud kitsch, nostalgia is a dominating theme. Broderick's analysis offers a subtle and incisive look at various manifestations of nostalgia from the "reactionary nostalgia" of *Blast From the Past* to a critique of "official attempts at reifying nuclear weapons technologies" in *Matinee*.

The final chapter in this book, Peter C. van Wyck's "American Monument: The Waste Isolation Pilot Plant," takes us from the contemporary nuclear landscape into the distant future by examining the effort to find a suitable "monument" to mark the Waste Isolation Pilot Plant site—one that, van Wyck writes, will "perform the threat that lies beneath" for at least 10,000 years. Like Goin's examination of past and present nuclear sites, van Wyck contemplates a future monument that will serve its purpose to warn future generations of the danger buried in the desert and commemorate—but not celebrate—the history it must somehow record.

As contributors to the first book in the University Press of Colorado's *Atomic History and Culture* series, the authors recognize their own inclusion in Post Atomic Culture. We also hope that our basic structure will open a dialogue and that the book, by providing a sample of what atomic scholars are studying, will attract more scholarship to the field.

NOTES

1. Paul Boyer, *By the Bomb's Early Light: American Thought and Culture at the Dawn of the Atomic Age* (New York: Pantheon, 1985), xvii.

2. Allan M. Winkler, *Life Under a Cloud: American Anxiety About the Atom* (Urbana: University of Illinois Press, 1993).

3. The atomic library is constantly expanding. Examples of these topics include Michael A. Amundson, *Yellowcake Towns: Uranium Mining Communities in the American West* (Boulder: University Press of Colorado, 2002); Peter Bacon Hales, *Atomic Spaces: Living on the Manhattan Project* (Urbana: University of Illinois Press, 1997); Paul Loeb, *Nuclear Culture: Living and Working in the World's Largest Atomic Complex* (Philadelphia: New Society, 1986); Michele Stenehjem Gerber, *On the Home Front: The Cold War Legacy of the Hanford Nuclear Site,* 2nd ed. (Lincoln: University of Nebraska Press,

1997); Len Ackland, *Making a Real Killing: Rocky Flats and the Nuclear West* (Albuquerque: University of New Mexico Press, 1999); A. Costandina Titus, *Bombs in the Backyard: Atomic Testing and American Politics,* 2nd ed. (Reno: University of Nevada Press, 2001); Tad Bartimus and Scott McCartney, *Trinity's Children: Living Along America's Nuclear Highway* (Albuquerque: University of New Mexico Press, 1991); Kenneth D. Rose, *One Nation Underground: The Fallout Shelter in American Culture* (New York: New York University Press, 2001); Elaine Tyler May, *Homeward Bound: American Families in the Cold War* (New York: Basic, 1988); Eileen Welsome, *The Plutonium Files: America's Secret Medical Experiments in the Cold War* (New York: Dial, 1999); Bruce Hevley and John M. Findlay, *The Atomic West* (Seattle: University of Washington Press, 1998); John Bradley, ed., *Learning to Glow: A Nuclear Reader* (Tucson: University of Arizona Press, 2000); Alison Scott and Christopher Geist, eds., *The Writing on the Cloud: American Culture Confronts the Atomic Bomb* (Lanham, MD: University Press of America, 1997).

4. Carla Freccero, *Popular Culture: An Introduction* (New York: New York University Press, 1999), 1–12.

5. John Fiske, *Understanding Popular Culture* (Boston: Unwin Hyman, 1989), 23.

6. Winkler, *Life Under a Cloud,* 27.

7. Ibid., 28.

8. Several atomic case studies examine this shift including ibid.; Titus, *Bombs in the Backyard*; and Ackland, *Making a Real Killing.*

9. The Simpson's online archive is a good place to begin research on the show; see http://www.snpp.com/ [accessed October 14, 2002].

10. The *Enola Gay* controversy is covered in Martin Harwit, *An Exhibit Denied: Lobbying the History of Enola Gay* (New York: Copernicus, 1996), and Edward T. Linenthal and Tom Engelhardt, *History Wars: The Enola Gay and Other Battles for the American Past* (New York: Metropolitan Books/Henry Holt, 1996). The National Atomic Museum home page can be found at http://www.atomicmuseum.com/ [accessed October 14, 2002]. Its gift shop controversy can be found at http://www.motherjones.com/mustreads/090699.html [accessed October 14, 2002]. The Bureau of Atomic Tourism can be accessed at www.atomictourist.com [accessed October 14, 2002].

CHAPTER ONE

Atomic Comics

The Comic Book Industry Confronts the Nuclear Age

FERENC M. SZASZ

American contributions to the world's popular culture have been legion: Hollywood, jazz, the blues, country music, and rock and roll; Coca Cola, Pepsi Cola, and Dr. Pepper; Corn Flakes, Grape Nuts, Graham Crackers, and Twinkies; Josephine Baker, Louis Armstrong, Dolly Parton, and Elvis Presley, just to name a few. Newspaper comic strips and the lowly comic book belong at the top of any such list. From humble beginnings, they emerged during the post–World War I era to become a force of unprecedented social power.

Knowledgeable critics have long recognized the impact of the comics. One authority has argued that comics were "the single most significant [mass] medium for our youth in the 1940s and 1950s," and another has claimed that until the popular appeal of television in the early 1960s, "the comic book was the dominant element of the culture of American children."[1] Recently, the Smithsonian Institution acknowledged the importance of comics with two official book compilations, and in 1995 the Library of Congress featured a popular exhibit celebrating a century of cartoon art.[2] After years of neglect, the oft-scorned comic book is finally getting its due.

With their garish covers, minimal text, and powerful sequential imagery, comic books played a vital role in explaining the nuclear age to American readers. During the half century from 1945 forward, the comic book industry depicted atomic themes in four overlapping phases. For about a decade after the close of World War II, comic artists and editors confronted the ambivalent nature of the atomic era with considerable skill. Writers in these years acknowledged the horrors of Hiroshima and Nagasaki, plus the dangers of nuclear war, but they balanced them with hopes for great advances through peaceful uses of atomic energy. In the second phase, from roughly 1950 to roughly 1970, comic books largely shed this approach to depict a hard-line Cold War standoff between the United States and the Soviet Union. In the third phase, comic artists from about 1965 to about 1989 drew on atomic themes chiefly as a means to give their heroes or villains super powers. During this period, however, two subcurrents emerged that forever altered the atomic/comic link. In the mid-1960s low-budget underground "comix" artists began to express absolute contempt for every aspect of the nuclear world. Then, in 1972, Japanese cartoonist Keiji Nakazawa published the initial installment of his now classic *Barefoot Gen,* a firsthand pictorial account of the Allied bombing of Hiroshima. After this, atomic comics assumed a multifaceted personality.

The outlines of the fourth, or "Contemporary," phase are far from clear. In fact, they reflect a convergence of all the previous themes in an "anything goes" atmosphere. Contemporary atomic comics include numerous atomic heroes, postapocalyptic nuclear tales, science fiction, millennial confrontations, pornography, spy intrigue, adventure stories, and bitter, sardonic humor. But during the last fifty years, at least three generations of readers have been shaped by very different comic book presentations of the nuclear world.

INITIAL REACTION

Since the comic book industry operated on a several-month lead time, the abrupt end of World War II in August 1945 caught the industry completely by surprise. For the most part, it was not until early 1946 that writers were able to come out with atomic comic stories. In January 1946 *Real Life Comics* placed an atomic bomb on its cover, but the issue lacked an interior story. An unnamed editor, however, wrote a lengthy introduction that set the tone for the next decade: "Most of today's leaders are already old. They will soon have to pass their leadership to younger hands. And when they pass it on it will be squarely up to the boys and girls now growing to manhood and womanhood in the post-war world to see that the tremendous force of the atom is used for the good of mankind."[3]

The foremost attempt to educate American youth in this fashion probably came with *Dagwood Splits the Atom* (1949). In this work King Features lent its familiar cartoon characters for a challenging assignment. Blondie and Dagwood shrank to atom size to explain nuclear fission through a combination of illustration and rather dense text, as Mandrake the Magician, Popeye, and Jiggs marveled at the Bumsteads' adventures. Newsman Bob Considine wrote the introduction, and none other than ex–Manhattan Project chief, General Leslie R. Groves (by then retired), wrote the foreword. Considine praised *Dagwood Splits the Atom* as the clearest explanation of atomic energy he had seen. He encouraged young people to choose atomic energy for their careers, predicting that the atom would eventually power trains, cars, and aircraft. General Groves seconded this sentiment. "No effort is too great for us to make in imparting the facts about atomic energy to the greatest number of our people," he wrote. King Features artist Joe Musial dedicated the comic to the nation's young people. It was up to them to assume the responsibility of directing atomic energy toward useful purposes, he stated. Musial also cautioned readers that the knowledge of how to split the atom would never disappear. Since this publication was "no ordinary comic book," Musial urged people to read *Dagwood Splits the Atom* several times.[4]

In spite of this promising start, the educational wing of the comic book industry never performed as well as expected. One may assume that parents purchased the rather turgid *Dagwood Splits the Atom* far more frequently than children did. Still, from 1945 to 1950, editors and artists often focused on the ambivalence of atomic power and urged young people to use it with caution. Thus, the initial comic book response to the onset of the atomic age proved surprisingly perceptive.

Simultaneously, the various comic companies created a bevy of new superheroes to confront the atom. In late fall 1945 Jay Burtis Publications boldly featured a caped, shirtless, masked hero wearing bathing trunks on the cover of its *Atomic Bomb* comic book. Although he dominated the cover, Mr. "Atomic Bomb" made no appearance inside. There was no second issue.[5]

After this false start, three other companies also attempted to market an "atomic superhero" in 1945 and 1946. In American Boy's Comics' November–December 1945 *Headline Comics,* the hero, "Adam Mann," accidentally drank a glass of heavy water into which some U^{235} crystals had fallen and then stumbled into a high-voltage machine. This "incredible chemical accident" turned Adam Mann into a human atomic bomb, with the new power concentrated exclusively in his right hand. (He had to wear a lead glove to contain the radioactivity.) Donning a red cape, a kilt, and what appears to be a Roman Legionnaire's helmet, "Atomic Man" spent his efforts righting various wrongs, such as thwarting a deranged scientist who planned to take over the world. After dispatching

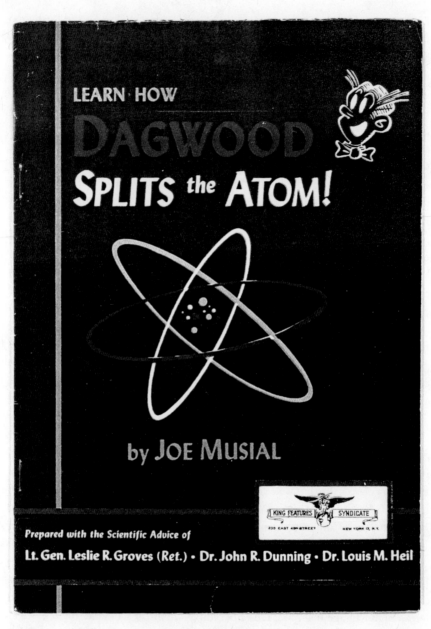

1.1 Dagwood Splits the Atom *(1949), with an introduction by General Leslie R. Groves, attempted to explain atomic energy and simultaneously urge young people to choose nuclear-related careers. Reprinted with special permission of King Features Syndicate.*

the villain, Atomic Man berated him for "using [his] scientific knowledge for destructive purposes."[6] In the course of his career in *Headline Comics,* Atomic Man announced that he "would use my power to crush every evil influence in the world."[7] Unfortunately, Atomic Man used his power for only six issues; the title expired in September 1946.

Other atomic heroes suffered similar fates. Regor Company's *Atomic Thunderbolt* hit the newsstands in February 1946 with the story of William Burns, former merchant mariner, who had degenerated into "Willy the Wharf Rat" after suffering shell shock from a near-miss by a Nazi torpedo. A fiendish scientist enticed Willy into his laboratory for an experiment but mistakenly pulled the wrong lever. The ensuing blast killed the scientist but left Willy with an indestructible body and the ability to fly. Garbed in white costume and red gloves with a sun symbol on his chest, the *Atomic Thunderbolt* resolved to "devote my life to save mankind from itself." Achieving this goal proved difficult, as the *Atomic Thunderbolt* did not survive for a second issue.[8]

His successor, *Atoman,* fared only slightly better. Spark Publications prefaced its 1946 comic with two pages of nuclear history, reminding readers that atomic power could be used for both good and evil. The artists then unveiled a masked, yellow-caped hero whose story "comes right out of the headlines." Scientist Barry Dale worked at the "Atomic Institute" studying "the secret atomic formula." In a manner never fully explained, he became radioactive and acquired new strength as *Atoman,* a person "whose body generates atomic power." The tale concluded with a soliloquy: "Atomic power cannot belong to one man . . . group of men . . . or even one nation! It belongs to the whole world! My own power must be used to help all people . . . regardless of race or creed or nationality."[9] *Atoman* lasted only two issues, expiring in April 1946.

The more established comic book superheroes, such as Superman, Wonder Woman, and the Marvel family, discovered that the atomic bomb matched even their powers. This made for some awkward storytelling. In an October 1946 *Action* 101 story, Superman was forced to swallow a drug that made him temporarily insane. (He did this only to save Lois Lane's life.) In this befuddled state, he mistakenly flew into the 1946 Bikini atomic blast, which, fortunately, cleared his mind. In gratitude, Superman borrowed a camera to photograph the mushroom cloud from above as "a warning to men who talk against peace."[10] In radio and film incarnations, Superman regularly confronted a villain named "Atom Man," and his well-known vulnerability to kryptonite surely resonated with readers as "radioactivity."[11]

Captain Marvel Adventures provided probably the most imaginative comic book treatment of atomic themes in the immediate postwar era. Most of the

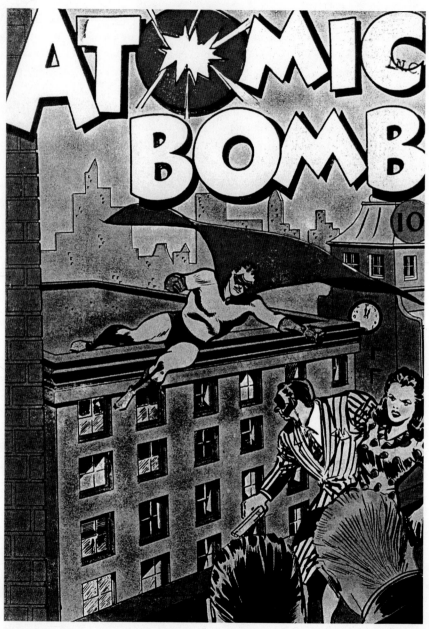

1.2 The Jay Burtis Company's Atomic Bomb *emerged as the first comic book "atomic hero" (Fall 1945), but he failed to survive for a second issue. Author's collection.*

almost 500 Captain Marvel stories were written by former pulp fiction writer Otto Binder and were usually drawn by master artist C. C. Beck. They combined their talents to create a kindly, obtuse, even whimsical superhero whose sales eventually topped those of Superman in the late 1940s. (His enemies called him "the Big Red Cheese.")

Binder and Beck crafted a number of Captain Marvel "atomic parables." In October 1946 Captain Marvel confronted the onset of atomic war. The cover depicts him vainly attempting to halt two incoming atomic bombs. In the story, Beck drew the destruction of Chicago and the death of a mother and child whom Captain Marvel had just rescued from a burning house. "Everyone died in this atomic war!" the hero despairs. "I'm . . . I'm the only man left alive." Fortunately, the story proves to be only a television dramatization. In the last panel the children watching the show realize that "we'd all better learn to live and get along together . . . one nation with all other nations . . . and one person with all other persons so that the terrible Atomic War will never occur!"[12]

In another story Captain Marvel resolves a conflict between ants and wasps, who were on the verge of an atomic war to decide which species would dominate the globe. (Because of their size, the ants had slipped through the U.S. defense plants to steal atomic secrets. In turn, the wasps had stolen the secrets from the ants.) In solving this dispute, Captain Marvel helped the ants and wasps form the "UI"—a United Insects organization: "Like our United Nations, it will promote peace here in your insect civilization!"[13]

In 1951 Captain Marvel battled an "atomic fire" that could not be extinguished on earth. He solved the problem by cutting out a 100-mile flaming circle of soil and flinging it into the sun. In the last panel, the indestructible hero nearly collapses at the realization that if he had failed, it would have been the end of the world.[14]

Shortly afterward, Al Fago's *Atomic Mouse* and *Atomic Rabbit* emerged as the chief postwar "atomic animals." Born in 1953, meek "Cimota" Mouse was badly treated until he swallowed some U^{235} pills, donned cape and costume (with a large "A" on the chest), and reversed his forename. Afterward, he assumed a new role: "helping to keep peace and order through[out] the universe." Lighthearted and cleverly drawn, the atomic-powered Mouse lasted fifty-four issues, with both television and movie tie-ins.[15]

Two years later Fago's artists tried to replicate this success by creating *Atomic Rabbit*, who gained his powers from munching radioactive carrots. On a 1957 *Atomic Rabbit* cover "the President" proclaimed that "Atomic Rabbit is the fastest and most powerful crusader for law and order in the world."[16] The name was changed to *Atomic Bunny* the next year, but the atomic rabbit hero disappeared after only nineteen issues. In their lighthearted fashion, these atomic animals probably helped neutralize the earlier fears represented by such villains as "Mr. Atom" and others. Still, none of the initial postwar "atomic" characters, human or animal, had long careers. Perhaps the ambivalence that dominated the late 1940s atomic culture could not be expressed in the restricted form of a costumed, comic book superhero.

THE COLD WAR ERA, 1950–1975

In 1949 America's nuclear monopoly ended when the Soviet Union detonated its first atomic weapon. Shortly afterward, naturalized British scientist Klaus Fuchs was arrested and convicted of passing atomic secrets to Soviet agents. Simultaneously, Harry S Truman gave the go-ahead for America's hydrogen bomb program and selected the Nevada Test Site, northeast of Las Vegas, as the primary continental location for nuclear testing. Until the moratorium of 1958 and the Partial Test Ban Treaty of 1963, the United States detonated over 100 aboveground tests at the Nevada Test Site.[17]

The Cold War tensions of the 1950s made their way into the comic format, but after 1954 the industry imposed strict new guidelines as to what material could be depicted. This came about only after considerable pressure from parents' groups, social critics, and the U.S. government. Congress actually held a special hearing on the "menace" of comic books.

To protect itself, the industry (Dell and Classics excepted) established a self-regulatory body, the Comics Code Authority, and hastily terminated the worst offenders of the day—crime and horror books. After 1954, few retailers would carry any comic that did not bear the proper seal of approval. This self-censorship lasted until the emergence of "underground comix" in the mid-1960s and the accompanying shift in mainstream public tolerance a decade or so later.[18]

The 1954 Comics Code Authority forbade portrayal of kidnapping, hidden weapons, vampires, overt sexuality, horror stories, disrespect for authority, and similar themes. But it said nothing about atomic weapons.[19] Consequently, the industry drew on the nuclear themes of the day with regularity. The fascination with atomic espionage, as reflected in the trial and conviction of Fuchs in Britain, led to *Atomic Spy Cases* (Spring 1950). In the lead story (set in Nevada) foreign villains came close to escaping with "the formula," but in the end "our nation's secret remains safe!" Although no second *Atomic Spy Cases* ever appeared, the subsequent trial and execution of Julius and Ethel Rosenberg for passing nuclear secrets to the Soviets fueled such popular 1950s titles as *Spy Hunters, Spy Thrillers,* and *Spy Cases.*

1.3 Al Fago's *cleverly drawn* Atomic Rabbit, *with his esteemed colleague,* Atomic Mouse, *helped neutralize the nation's nuclear fears during the Cold War years of the 1950s. Charlton.*

The increasing tension with the Soviet Union soon provided the main grist for the industry's mill. Indeed, Cold War "Atomic Combat" themes remained a staple for comic book artists and writers for over four decades. In 1952 St. John Publishers produced five issues of *Atom-Age Combat*. In 1958 Fago magazines published two issues under an identical title, which caused St. John to revive its own publication. In this latter version, the text announced that "this is the Atom Age! The unbelievable has already begun to come true."[20] Although *Atom-Age Combat* stated that its stories were factual, not science fiction, the editors had their categories reversed. Virtually every issue contained some form of science fiction adventure tale. In one story the hero discovered that the enemy were actually Martians.[21]

Throughout the 1950s, nuclear explosions appeared on over twenty-six comic book covers and in scores of large interior "splash panels." Although comics artists often drew atomic explosions and devastated cities, because of the code they never depicted actual death scenes. Similarly, they never mentioned fallout or radiation sickness. Moreover, artists frequently depicted soldiers or civilians and atomic explosions in the same panel. In one tale Captain America watches a Nevada explosion from close range. In another, Rex, the Wonder Dog, saves his family from a Nevada blast by leading them to a nearby cave.[22] Yet another tale shows navy frogmen swimming within yards of the base of a mushroom cloud.

The "atomic war" books of the 1950s provided the most graphic horror tales of the era. The titles *Atomic War* and *World War III* created a very grim world, as they depicted "the war that will never happen if America remains strong and alert." One cover showed U.S. aircraft unleashing hydrogen bombs over the Kremlin in revenge for the destruction of New York, Chicago, and Detroit. Other stories solemnly discussed "the atomic exchange" of 1960. One tale contained such memorable lines as "Amerikanski, I'll get you. . . . Aargh" and "Yiiii . . . It's the end of the world." These series expired after only a few issues.[23] For obvious reasons, the theme of atomic conflagration had limited long-term dramatic potential.

ATOMIC SUPERHEROES, 1960–1980s

The appearance of several new atomic-related superheroes in the 1960s provided welcome relief from the previous decade's tales of nuclear destruction. During this period a revived Atom (1961), Captain Atom (1960), Dr. Solar (1960), Spiderman (1962), and Firestorm, the Nuclear Man (1978) breathed new life into the atoms-for-justice ethos. A good many of their foes also had nuclear connections.

Virtually everyone agrees that the greatest atomic character of the 1960s was Spiderman. Created in 1962 by writer Stan Lee and artist Steve Ditko, Marvel's Spiderman became the most popular costumed hero of the next two decades. The story drew on familiar themes, but with a light, artistic touch. Peter Parker, a shy high school student, attended a public science exhibit on radiation. A spider fell into the demonstrator's "radioactive ray gun" beam and bit Parker just before it expired. Through this means, Parker acquired the spider's proportional strength—including the ability to climb walls—plus a sixth sense, a "spider sense" that tingles in the presence of danger.

Like Superman and Captain America before him, Spiderman became a cultural icon for his era. Somehow the figure of an angst-ridden, quasi-nuclear costumed hero filled a social need in the 1960s and 1970s. Perhaps this was a result of the breakdown of the Cold War consensus of the 1950s, or perhaps it could be traced to increased anxiety over the arms race and the growing quagmire of Vietnam. Whatever the reasons, by the mid-1960s Spiderman's sales topped those of Superman. In 1965 *Esquire* magazine observed that Spiderman was as popular in radical campus circles as revolutionary leader Che Guevara.[24]

In a 1993 reminiscence, Stan Lee confessed that from a writer's point of view, it had become increasingly difficult to devise believable circumstances to give superheroes their powers. It should not be surprising that "atomic radiation" began to fill this role in a number of guises. D.C.'s "Negative Man," a member of the popular "super freaks" of the *Doom Patrol,* boasted such an origin. Similarly, Marvel's *The Incredible Hulk* was originally physicist Dr. Bruce Banner, who stumbled into a nuclear explosion. Likewise, Spiderman's foe, nuclear scientist Otto Octavius, was turned into the evil "Dr. Octopus" when an atomic accident welded metal tentacles to his body.[25]

In addition to these new atomic-related characters, the more established superheroes wrestled with atomic dangers and battled nuclear villains on a semiregular basis from the 1960s to the present. Such stories became so common that those described here will have to serve as representative of a genre that still continues: in *Showcase* 23 (1960) Green Lantern thwarts an invisible villain from detonating an atomic bomb. Four years later *The Flash* (May 1964) drew on his super speed to keep a nuclear bomb from obliterating a city. In 1965 Superman's hands became coated with invisible chemicals so that one clap would trigger an atomic explosion. In *Adventure Comics* 442 (November-December 1975) Aquaman barely stopped a nuclear missile.[26] The list could easily be extended.

For over two decades the industry also periodically dealt with the theme of an all-out nuclear conflagration. The cover of the September-October 1970

Strange Adventures wondered which of the eight nations with H-bombs (in "1986") would trigger World War III.[27] D.C. artists often depicted Superman or Superboy wrestling with similar themes. In 1983 they previewed "The Great Atomic War of 1986," and the next year they highlighted "the day they nuked Superman." In 1985 Superman declared in anguish, "They did it. They finally had a nuclear war. And nobody survived except me!"[28] This theme continues today: both *Captain America* (December 1998) and *The Adventures of Superman* (February 1999) sported elaborate "Nuclear Nightmare" covers.

THE COMIX REVOLUTION, 1960–1990

The emergence of the counterculture of the 1960s clashed head-on with the restraints imposed by the Comics Code Authority. Reacting to what one scholar has termed "the most severe form of censorship applied to any mass medium," young underground artists rebelled to create a bold new form of sequential art in their "Comix."[29] In retrospect, comix served as an ideal mass medium by which to express cultural dissent. They could be produced cheaply in a basement or garage, and their visual images had great appeal to a generation raised with television.

The most important antinuclear comix figure of the 1970s was probably San Francisco cartoonist Leonard Rifas. In *All-Atomic Comics* (1976) Rifas launched a severe attack on the nuclear power industry. When he began the project four years earlier, Rifas noted, he had planned to present a "balanced" view of the issue, but he soon abandoned that approach. The narrator for *All-Atomic Comics* is a three-legged frog, and the story line is periodically interrupted with "Fun Facts to Know and Tell About Nuclear Power." These "facts" speak of the 1974 death of Karen Silkwood just before she planned to reveal falsification of safety reports at the plutonium plant where she worked, the mutation of frogs from waste dumped by the Amsterdam Nuclear Research Institute in Holland, and the building of Colorado homes on uranium tailings. "Is Nuclear Power the Answer?" asks a figure on the front cover. The snappy reply: "Kid, I'd Bet Your Life on It!"[30] The book went through five printings and sold about 50,000 copies, a high number for an underground publication.

Shortly afterward Rifas founded a company, Educomics, to further his antinuclear message. Educomics distributed a variety of antinuclear comics from abroad, such as *Nuclear Komics* (the Philippines), *Rumbles* (Canada), *Atomic Horror Comic* (Australia), and the *Internationalist* (Australia). Educomics also produced issue-oriented comics on a variety of contemporary social concerns including *Energy Comics*, which focused on alternative energy sources, and *Food Comics*, which analyzed the dangers and inequalities of the present system of food distribution.

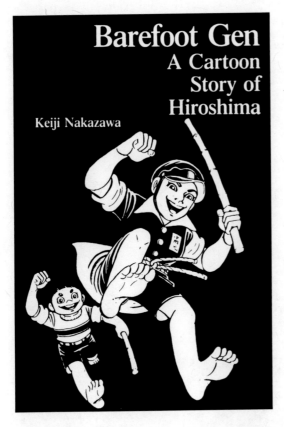

Barefoot Gen
A Cartoon
Story of
Hiroshima

Keiji Nakazawa

1.4a During the 1970s, Japanese cartoonist Keiji Nakazawa, who had lived through the bombing of Hiroshima as a child, published a four-volume, semi-autobiographical account of his family's experiences. Barefoot Gen *probably ranks as the most famous comic book in Japanese history.* Courtesy, *Keiji Nakazawa.*

In addition to *All-Atomic Comics,* Rifas oversaw the first American publication of Keiji Nakazawa's comic book retelling of the story of Hiroshima.[31] In September 1972 Nakazawa published a semiautobiographical account of the atomic attack on Hiroshima in the popular Japanese comic *Shonen Gam.* The editors encouraged Nakazawa (who had lived through the blast and lost a father, brother, and sister to it) to expand his story. Working feverishly over the next two years, the cartoonist produced a multivolume cartoon book, *Barefoot Gen* ("Gen" means fundamental particle, source, or, more loosely, "Everyman"). The story proved so compelling that a special, largely volunteer company arose to translate *Barefoot Gen* into French, German, Swedish, Norwegian, Indonesian, Portuguese, Russian, and Esperanto.[32] A four-volume English version was completed in 1994.[33]

Throughout the books, Nakazawa is as harsh on the Japanese militarists who led the nation into war as he is on the Americans. Although not strictly autobiographical, *Barefoot Gen* contains enough firsthand flavor to give it great power. Nakazawa has devoted his entire professional cartooning career to depicting nuclear themes. *Barefoot Gen* remains the most famous comic ever published in Japan.

Although *Barefoot Gen* has often been compared with American artist Art Spiegelman's *Maus*—a gripping cartoon study of the holocaust—as an example

ONE OF THOSE SEVEN, NAMED THE "ENOLA GAY" AFTER THE MOTHER OF THE PILOT, LOADED WITH THE ATOMIC BOMB "LITTLE BOY" WAS BEING READIED FOR TAKEOFF.

AT 1:35 AM THREE WEATHER RECONNAISSANCE PLANES TOOK OFF FOR HIROSHIMA, THE NUMBER ONE TARGET CITY, AND REPORTED "IDEAL WEATHER"; IT WAS DECIDED THEN TO DROP THE ATOMIC BOMB ON HIROSHIMA.

THE DROPPING OF THE BOMB WAS FIXED FOR 9:15 AM (8:15 JAPANESE TIME) ON AUG. 6TH.

AT 2:45 AM, THE "ENOLA GAY" TOOK OFF FROM THE BASE IN THE MARIANA ISLANDS, FOLLOWED BY TWO RECONNAISSANCE PLANES...

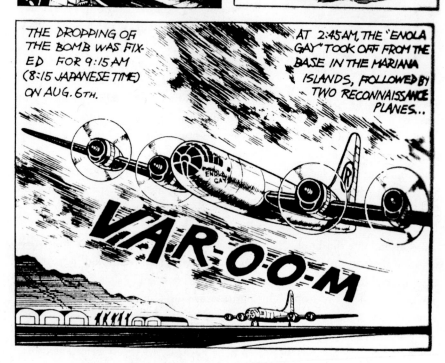

1.4b Barefoot Gen. Courtesy, *Keiji Nakazawa*.

A TERRIBLE FATE WAS HEADED FOR GEN'S CITY OF HIROSHIMA.

of the power unleashed by the "new comics," it has never garnered the same popular recognition in the United States. Spiegelman received a special Pulitzer Prize for *Maus,* but Nakazawa's work is recognized only by specialists.

Without exception, both Japanese cartoonists and the underground artists of the 1960s and 1970s depicted nuclear history and the nuclear world in the darkest possible terms. In their eyes the term *atomic* was synonymous with "man's inhumanity to man."

THE CONTEMPORARY ERA, 1985–PRESENT

The overall pattern of contemporary atomic comics is not yet clear. There is general agreement, however, that comic books play a much smaller role in shaping youth culture than they did in previous generations. Television, computers, and increasingly sophisticated video games have given the comics industry stiff competition.

The end of the Cold War in 1989 took the edge off comic depiction of nuclear villains or atomic holocaust. Current concerns, such as nuclear waste disposal and nuclear arms reduction, lack dramatic potential. No educational comic has attempted to deal with the largely successful story of nuclear medicine. The only remaining nuclear theme with dramatic cachet seems to be nuclear terrorism. Crusade Comics' *Atomik Angels,* a team of smart-talking teenagers trained for "nuclear crisis intervention," addressed this concern. The team's attitude is decidedly flip—"even the smallest atomic blast can just about ruin your day!"—and the stories include few genuine atomic connections.[34]

Although a number of contemporary American comics boast nuclear titles, seldom do they have any authentic nuclear content. *Reactor Girl* (1992), *Sub-Atomic Shock* (1993), *Quantum Leap* (1992), and *Atomic City Tales* all go their own (nonatomic) ways. *Atomic Chili* (1990) is a collection of graphic horror tales. *Dr. Radium: Man of Science* (1992) contains only the odd nuclear allegory. *Post Nuke Dick* is a heavy-handed satire set in a postholocaust world. *Bulletin From Ground Zero* treats sexual innuendo, and all the issues of *A-Bomb* are sexually explicit. The four-volume *Atomic Age* and *Fusion* rank as pure science fiction. The 1999 *Adam Bomb* is only a campy adventure tale.

All this suggests that at the dawn of the twenty-first century, atomic-themed comic book stories have become as familiar to American readers as fast food. They are so familiar, in fact, that industry writers and artists are no longer able to tap into them for sustained dramatic development.

Modern comic book illustrators might still rely on radiation to create their superheroes, but they now do so in a lighthearted vein. In 1986 Kevin Eastman and Peter Laird created their popular *Teenage Mutant Ninja Turtles* to parody

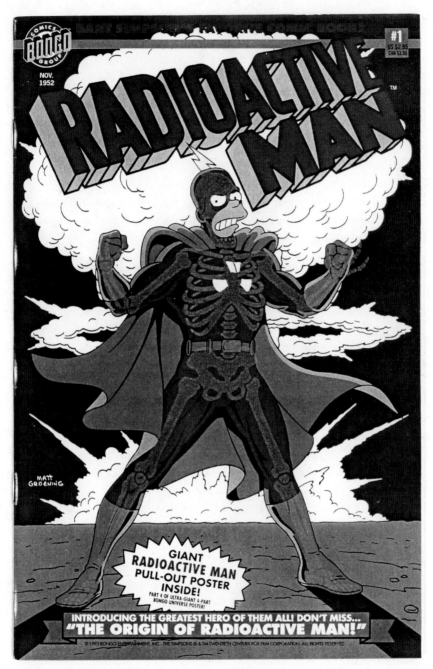

1.5 The bumbling Radioactive Man, *aided by his faithful sidekick, Fallout Boy, races about defending "authority." Matt Groening's combination of humor and satirical nihilism regarding the contemporary atomic scene resonates with many young people today. Bongo Entertainment.*

the superhero genre. The turtles acquired much of their power from inundation by a "flowing ooze."[35] The *Adolescent Radioactive Black Belt Hamsters* (1986), a parody of a parody, received their power from radioactive jello. One also finds mention of *Colossal Nuclear Bambino Samurai Snails* and *Radioactive Wrestling Rodents.*

By far the most creative parody is Matt Groening's *Radioactive Man.* True to tradition, Groening's hero missed the sign warning of an explosion at the Nevada Test Site and became engulfed in an atomic blast. The result was "this brightly-garbed champion of justice, this defender of the USA, the enemy of non-conformity, this Radioactive Man." With his sidekick "Fallout Boy," the rather dense Radioactive Man goes about defending "authority." Groening's satires reflect the comix nihilistic view of all things nuclear while also being a thorough send-up of comic book history.[36]

To go from *Real Life*'s urgent plea in 1945 that American youth use the atom wisely to the outrageous bumbling of Radioactive Man in the twenty-first century is to travel a considerable distance. Although no single artistic medium—film, art, fiction, song, theater, sculpture, photography, or history—can encompass the entirety of the atomic story, for over fifty years comic books have done their best to depict the various facets of the nuclear world.

Like all aspects of popular culture, the last five decades of atomic comics reflect a quicksilver world in terms of analysis. Universal medium though it may be, the shifting nature of the comic book nuclear message defies precise definition. Still, only the hardened cynic would argue that millions of people could read these various atomic comic stories and remain unaffected.

Historian Arthur Berger has strong views on this matter. He argues that comic book reading played a key role in the socialization of young people for their specific generation "by virtue of the simple fact that millions of children—and adults—cannot continually be exposed to a form of communication without something happening."[37] Thus, it surely made a difference if a young person were raised on themes of atomic ambivalence, hopes for endless nuclear power, atomic-powered heroes, hard-edged defense measures, or bitter contempt for all things nuclear. The atomic comic message absorbed during one's youth is likely to resonate for a lifetime.

NOTES

I thank Robert Del Tredici, Maria Szasz, and Nathan Wilson for their assistance in the preparation of this manuscript.

1. Ernst and Mary Gerber, comps., *The Photo-Journal Guide to Comic Books* (Minden, NV: Gerber, 1990), vol. 2, C-10; Dick Lupoff and Don Thompson, eds., *All in Color*

for a Dime, rev. ed. (Iola, WI: Krause; 1977), 11. Research in comic book history presents a number of challenges. Few university libraries hold comic collections, and some even refuse to accept them. Drawing on the industry trade journal, *Comics Buyer's Guide,* I spent several years compiling the books from which this chapter is drawn. One should also consult the annual (since 1970) *Overstreet Comic Book Price Guide,* which conveys much more than the title suggests, and the excellent two-volume study by Ernest and Mary Gerber, *The Photo-Journal Guide to Comic Books.* See also the essay by M. Thomas Inge, "Comic Books," in *Handbook of American Popular Culture,* ed. M. Thomas Inge (New York: Greenwood, 1988), 74–99, and the collection of essays in M. Thomas Inge, *Comics as Culture* (Jackson: University Press of Mississippi, 1990). The literature is growing steadily, and among the best recent accounts are William J. Savage Jr., *Comic Books and America, 1945–1954* (Norman: University of Oklahoma Press, 1990); Nicky Wright, *The Classic Era of American Comics* (Chicago: Contemporary Books, 2000); and especially Bradford W. Wright, *Comic Book Nation: The Transformation of Youth Culture in America* (Baltimore: Johns Hopkins University Press, 2001).

2. Bill Blackbeard and Martin Williams, eds., *The Smithsonian Collection of Newspaper Comics* (Washington, DC, and New York: Smithsonian Institution Press and Harry N. Abrams, 1977); Martin Barrier and Martin Williams, eds., *A Smithsonian Book of Comic Book Comics* (Washington, DC, and New York: Smithsonian Institution Press and Harry N. Abrams, 1981); Stefan Kanfer, "From the Yellow Kid to Yellow Journalism," *Civilization: The Magazine of the Library of Congress* 1 (May-June 1995): 32–37. See also Jerry Robinson, *The Comics: An Illustrated History of Comic Strip Art* (New York: G. P. Putnam's Sons, 1974); Maurice Horn, ed., *100 Years of American Newspaper Comics* (New York: Gramercy, 1966); Bill Blackbeard and Dale Crain, eds., *The Comic Strip Century: Celebrating 100 Years of an American Art Form* (Englewood Cliffs, NJ: O. G. Publishing, 1995); Dennis Gifford, *The International Book of Comics* (Toronto: Royce, 1984).

3. *Real Life Comics* (January 1946), Nedor; quotation from inside front cover.

4. *Dagwood Splits the Atom* (1949), King Features. Such comic book depictions were much more sophisticated than the nuclear songs found in the country music of the era. See Charles Wolfe, "Nuclear Country: The Atomic Bomb in Country Music," *Journal of Country Music* 6 (January 1978): 4–22.

5. *Atomic Bomb* (1945), Jay Burtis.

6. *Headline Comics* (November-December 1945).

7. Ibid.

8. *The Atomic Thunderbolt* (February 1946), Regor.

9. *Atoman* 1 (February 1946), Spark.

10. *Action* 101 (October 1946), National Periodical Publications/Detective Comics.

11. These incarnations have been collected in *The Superman Radio Scripts: Superman vs. the Atom Man,* ed. Steven Korte (New York: Watson-Guptill, 2001).

12. *Captain Marvel Adventures* 66 (October 1946), Fawcett.

13. Savage, *Comic Books and America, 1945–1954,* 20–21.

14. *Captain Marvel Adventures* 122 (July 1951), Fawcett; see also *Captain Marvel Adventures* 131 (April 1952), Fawcett.

15. *Atomic Mouse* (December 1984), Charlton; reprint of 1953 stories.

16. *Atomic Rabbit* (August 1957), Charlton.

17. The best studies on this theme are Paul Boyer, *By the Bomb's Early Light: American Thought and Culture at the Dawn of the Atomic Age* (New York: Pantheon, 1980); Allan M. Winkler, *Life Under a Cloud: American Anxiety About the Atom* (New York: Oxford University Press, 1993); Spencer R. Weart, *Nuclear Fear: A History of Images* (Cambridge: Harvard University Press, 1986).

18. James Gilbert, *A Cycle of Outrage: American Reaction to the Juvenile Delinquent in the 1950s* (New York: Oxford University Press, 1986), 80; Roger Sabin, *Comics, Comix, and Graphic Novels* (London: Phardon, 1996), 68.

19. Greg S. McCue with Clive Bloom, *Dark Knights: The New Comics in Context* (London: Bluto, 1993).

20. *Atom-Age Combat* 1 (February 1958), St. John.

21. *Atom-Age Combat* 1 (March 1959), Fago.

22. *The Adventures of Rex the Wonder Dog* 11 (September–October 1953), National Comics.

23. *World War III,* 2 (May 1953), Ace; *Atomic War* 3 (February 1953), Jr.

24. Les Daniels, *Comix: A History of Comic Books in America* (New York: Bonanza, 1975), 139, for *Esquire* quotation. See also Les Daniels, *Marvel: Five Fabulous Decades of the World's Greatest Comics* (New York: Harry N. Abrams, 1991); Richard Reynolds, *Super Heroes: A Modern Mythology* (Jackson: University Press of Mississippi, 1992).

25. Stan Lee, "Introduction," in *The Uncanny X-Men Masterworks* (New York: Marvel, 1993), n.p.; Stan Lee, *The Incredible Hulk* (New York: Simon and Schuster, 1978); Mike Benton, *Superhero Comics of the Silver Age* (Dallas: Taylor, 1991), 20–22.

26. Other examples, compiled by Tim Collins, president of RTS Unlimited, include *Black Cat Mystery* 35; *Fighting Navy* 74; *Forbidden Worlds* 9; *Space Adventures* 9; *Weird Science* 5.

27. *Strange Adventures* 226 (September–October 1970), National Periodical Publishers, D.C.

28. *Superman* (June 1985), D.C.

29. Sabin, chapter 5, "Going Underground," *Comics, Comix, and Graphic Novels,* 92–129. See also M. Thomas Inge, "A Chronology of the Development of the American Comic Book," in Robert M. Overstreet, comp., *The Overstreet Comic Book Price Guide,* 27th ed. (New York: Avon, 1997), A-75.

30. *All-Atomic Comics* (1976), Educomics. See also Dale Luciano, "Before It's Too Late, an Interview With Leonard Rifas," *Comics Journal* (n.d.). Copy sent by Rifas and in author's possession.

31. Keiji Nakazawa, *Gen of Hiroshima* (1962), Educomics.

32. Frederick L. Schodt, *Dreamland Japan: Writings on Modern Manga* (Berkeley: Stone Bridge, 1996), 307.

33. Keiji Nakazawa, *Barefoot Gen,* four volumes in English with various subtitles (Philadelphia: New Society, 1987–1994).

34. See the section on "The 1990s" in Paul Sassienie, *The Comic Book* (London: Ebury, 1994), 117–131.

35. Kevin Eastman and Peter Laird, *Teenage Mutant Ninja Turtles* (Chicago: First Comics, 1986), 16.

36. *Radioactive Man* 1 (1993); *Bartman, With Radioactive Man* 3 (1994), Bongo.

37. Arthur Berger, "Comics and Culture," *Journal of Popular Culture* 5 (Fall 1971): 164–177, quotation on 164.

Reinventing Los Alamos

Code Switching and Suburbia at America's Atomic City

JON HUNNER

The atomic bomb thrust the United States into a totally new age, one full of promise and peril. Atomic energy dramatically altered the way the government operated, the military fought, the economy functioned, and ordinary people felt. Reacting to this new reality, people responded with new ways of living. They searched for ways to understand and live in the Atomic Age and in so doing created a new culture. One of the first places people accommodated the new nuclear world was at its birthplace in Los Alamos, New Mexico.

To explore how people switch from one way of living to another, we must turn to linguistics for a moment. When speaking, people often code switch, a linguistic term that refers to shifting from the dominant language to another language. Sometimes this shows that a person is sophisticated, that he or she can express himself or herself in more than one language. Other times code switching is needed so people can talk about something their own language is unable

This chapter is a revised version of a chapter from *Inventing Los Alamos: The Creation of Atomic Culture, 1943–1957* (forthcoming from University of Oklahoma Press), reprinted with the permission of University of Oklahoma Press.

to express with precision. At Los Alamos people code switched originally because the U.S. Army ordered them to do so.

In national security matters, people use code names to protect the identity of something that is vitally important. For example, during World War II, military police forbad anyone to mention Los Alamos. Instead, residents said "Project Y," "Site Y," or "the Hill." Additionally, personnel in the laboratory at Los Alamos did not speak openly about atomic bombs but referred instead to "the gadget" or "the gizmo."

Cultural code switching also occurs. Anyone who borrows ideas, beliefs, fashion styles, and food from another culture is code switching. For example, when the young democracy of the United States looked for a national architectural style in the late eighteenth century, it turned to the Greek Classical style. It architecturally code switched to ancient Greece to make the cultural connection with the best-known democracy of the Western world. At Los Alamos, on the border among Native American, Hispanic, and Anglo cultures and on the border between the scientifically known and unknown, cultural code switching helped the atomic pioneers adapt to the new and challenging age.

Faced for the first time with an atomic explosion, some witnesses had to culturally code switch to understand the event. When Dr. J. Robert Oppenheimer, the civilian director of the laboratory at Los Alamos, experienced the first atomic detonation at Trinity in July 1945, he thought of Hindu scripture from the *Bhagavad-Gita*: "I am become Death, the destroyer of worlds."[1] In Hindu religion the god Shiva is eternally poised to destroy the earth at a moment's notice. Oppenheimer fully understood the physics behind the explosion, but he had to switch to Hinduism to grasp the moral and social implications of what he had helped unleash in the desert that morning.

As the town that invented nuclear weapons and the Atomic Age, Los Alamos holds a unique position in the creation of atomic culture. When the secrecy lifted after the bombing of Hiroshima, the nation's attention turned to the community and sought from this veiled town insights into the atomic future. During the first decade of nuclear policy, the federal government also looked to Los Alamos not just for new advances in nuclear weaponry but as a place to test civil defense strategies to survive those same weapons. In the early Cold War period, Los Alamos served as both a symbol for the promise of atomic energy and a test community to address some of the perils of nuclear weapons.

The U.S. Army created this top-secret post in response to scientific research originally conducted in Europe. In the 1930s European scientists including Enrico Fermi, Niels Bohr, Lise Meitner, Otto Hahn, and Fritz Strassmann revolutionized nuclear physics. These experiments culminated in

1938 when Hahn and Strassmann split uranium atoms with a release of an enormous amount of energy. Lacking an adequate word in physics to describe the phenomena, their colleague Meitner code switched a term from biology and called this process *fission,* an organic name for splitting a living organism in two.[2]

From 1943 to 1945 scientists, technicians, and military personnel at Los Alamos sought to harness the energy released from the split atom and to direct it into an explosive weapon. By 1945, 2,000 men and women were working at the laboratories at Los Alamos, with another 3,000 staff and family members residing at the army post on the Hill. This instant city of clapboard labs and Quonset hut homes housed some of the best scientific minds in the world. The homes, duplexes, quadroplexes, and apartments that housed the 5,000 residents were quickly built and not meant to last beyond the war. Electrical and water shortages, lack of adequate sewage disposal, paper-thin interior walls, and an abundance of mud all added to Americans' usual sacrifices with wartime rationing and overcrowding. At this top-secret community, scientists developed two operational types of atomic bombs using enriched uranium and plutonium. When the uranium-fueled Little Boy bomb fell on Hiroshima on August 6, 1945, the world changed overnight.

With the atomic bombing of Japan in August 1945, World War II ended. Even though the creation of an atomic weapon marked the successful end of its original mission, Los Alamos became a permanent town as the postwar nuclear arms race with the Soviet Union intensified. To provide for the atomic workers who remained after the war's end and to attract new personnel, the government invented suburban communities at its atomic facilities where none had existed before. At Los Alamos the postwar building boom solved three difficulties. First, it corrected a serious shortage of housing. Second, it invented an alternate image of Los Alamos for public scrutiny. And third, the new suburbs assisted lab personnel in adjusting to working and living in the shadow of the bomb. Residents on the Hill faced the challenges of the Atomic Age by code switching from a culture of shortages, military housing, and war to one of abundance, ranch houses, and suburban life.

In the summer of 1946 suburbia came to Los Alamos. Military officials approved spending $4.4 million for the construction of over 300 new homes in the Western Area on a plateau west of the original town. During the rest of the decade, hundreds of two- and three-bedroom ranch-style homes went up on the Hill and transformed the community. With modern appliances, attached carports, and enclosed lawns, the Western Area offered residents of Los Alamos homes comparable to those in new suburbs in other parts of the country. Additionally, a

2.1 During the early postwar period Los Alamos built the Western Area, an instant suburb, to attract personnel and offer a vision of an atomic utopia. Courtesy, *National Archives and Records Administration.*

$1.4 million shopping and community center replaced the old military Post Exchange with a modern facility that held retail stores and city offices. The postwar construction boom at Los Alamos created a modern suburb, both to house the families of lab personnel and to highlight the utopian aspect of the Atomic City.

From behind the fences, a new city on the Hill emerged that offered a shining example of the promise of nuclear energy for the contested history of Los Alamos. At times, the American public's support for nuclear weapons wavered, and to bolster that support, officials praised other applications of this new form of energy. As atomic historian Paul Boyer has noted, "Dreams of a

2.2 This modern duplex in the Western Area, with grass and lawn furniture, illustrates the move toward postwar normalcy at Los Alamos. Courtesy, *Los Alamos National Laboratory Archives.*

new 'world' of atomic energy just around the corner were a way of dealing with—or avoiding—unsettling realities: America's use of two atomic bombs to obliterate two cities and the prospect that even more terrible atomic weapons might someday devastate the earth."[3] As part of the drive for good publicity, local and national newspaper and magazine articles focused on the residential area of Los Alamos as it transformed itself into a model community.[4]

The mystique of the Atomic City, combined with its vital national security role, riveted the nation's attention. With public access to the top-secret laboratories at Los Alamos forbidden, the Atomic Energy Commission (AEC) censored the image of the site by focusing on the residential part of the town. Searching for the atomic bomb and prevented from seeing it because of the shield of secrecy, U.S. citizens saw the residential community instead. In the development of an atomic culture, the ultimate code switch inserted the suburban utopia of postwar Los Alamos for the terrifying image of a bomb capable of annihilating Japanese communities. By doing so, the AEC countered the American public's atomic fears for a while.

On August 29, 1949, the Soviet Union detonated its own nuclear weapon, and the dormant issue of civil defense against nuclear weapons awakened with a jolt. Several weeks after President Truman announced the detonation of the Soviet bomb, a laboratory official from Los Alamos offered this advice to Santa Fe's daily newspaper, the *New Mexican,* on what would happen to the Atomic City if a nuclear weapon struck:

> If you are within a half-mile of the point directly under an atomic explosion, you've had it. . . . From one-half to two miles from the explosion, it's all in the lap of lady luck. . . . At over two miles, the odds are way over on your side. So generally speaking, a bomb explosion over the present technical area here would raise the dickens with the tech area itself, the community center, and most of the residential area in the eastern end of Los Alamos.[5]

Despite this somewhat cheery appraisal of an atomic attack against Los Alamos, the threat to the laboratory and the community emerged as a real and ominous possibility.

These early public comments on the end of the U.S. atomic monopoly gave rise to a string of civil defense strategies. Federal, state, and local officials, scientists, medical doctors, journalists, and the general public all wrestled with what to do if one's neighborhood became ground zero. Los Alamos played a key role in transforming the military, technological, and political activities of the Cold War. Additionally, events at Los Alamos also influenced the country's cultural and social history, as individuals and communities sought ways to survive an atomic attack.

The country began debating the effects of atomic weapons on U.S. cities immediately after Hiroshima and Nagasaki. As early as August 12, 1945, journalist Edward R. Murrow said on his radio program, "Seldom if ever has a war ended leaving the victors with such a sense of uncertainty and fear, with such a realization that the future is obscure and that survival is not assured."[6] The U.S. Army report on the atomic bombing, *The Effects of the Atomic Bombs on Hiroshima and Nagasaki,* detailed the wide range of destructive energies from the bombs.[7] The bombs released devastating blast waves and intense heat (which caused deadly firestorms), as well as radiation that claimed tens of thousands of lives. Tens of thousands of people died at the moment of the blasts (or soon thereafter), and tens of thousands more succumbed over the following months and years from the lingering effects of the bombs' radiation. The *Bombing Survey,* as the report was called, established much of the foundation for civil defense responses and strategies in the High Cold War period.

Once the Soviets obtained atomic weapons, U.S. civil defense had to develop new strategies to face the threat. Responding to the awesome destructive power of an atomic blast and the evolving information about the dangers of radioactivity, in December 1950 the federal government reorganized its Office of Civilian Mobilization to become the Federal Civil Defense Administration (FCDA). The FCDA's mission included "coping with disaster on a scale neither this country nor any other country has before dreamed possible. The newer organization, when completed, must deal with all phases of such things as emergency housing, sanitation, rehabilitation, fire fighting, and radiation detection and treatment."[8] To emphasize the danger, the *Annual Report for 1951 of the Federal Civil Defense Administration* stated that the new dimension of atomic weapons "makes our backyards of today the potential front lines of tomorrow."[9] With one's barbecue pit a potential ground zero, civil defense efforts organized on local and national levels.

At the same time the AEC was creating a modern suburb at Los Alamos, civil defense directors in northern New Mexico prepared the public for a nuclear war. On January 10, 1951, the directors assembled in Los Alamos and agreed to form a mutual aid committee "to work out problems involved in the event of an attack on any of the critical target areas of the state."[10] The next night another civil defense meeting occurred, this time in nearby Española, to set up an emergency evacuation center. The meeting also called for volunteers to survey housing in the Española Valley "to determine how many people could be fed and housed in case of emergency."[11] Before the end of January, an additional meeting in Santa Fe ordered a survey of housing in the event of an evacuation. Since only one community in northern New Mexico could be considered a critical target area, the communities surrounding Los Alamos prepared to receive refugees from the Hill if the Soviets launched an atomic strike against the Atomic City.

Addressing individual civil defense issues, a flurry of stories appeared in local newspapers in January 1951 on how to survive an atomic bombing. Santa Fe's Civil Defense Public Information chairman, Joe M. Clark, wrote a series of articles and advised the public in the event of an atomic blast to "fall flat on your face. More than half of all wounds are the result of being bodily tossed about or struck by falling and flying objects."[12] In another article Clark assured readers that "people are not very likely to be exposed to dangerous amounts of [radioactivity] in most atomic raids."[13] Returning to a theme that first arose in the aftermath of Hiroshima and Nagasaki, Clark denied that any health hazards resulted from blasts at high altitudes, since most lingering radioactivity rode upward on the violent surge of super-hot gases; however, enough of a threat existed that in another of Clark's stories he warned the public to keep doors and windows closed in the event of an attack, since "it [was] far easier to prevent radioactive pollution of a household than it [was] to remove it."[14] As a response to the escalating arms race, Clark's advice created the impression that surviving a nuclear attack relied merely on planning and common sense, with little difference from a conventional attack.

Clark's articles in the *New Mexican* supported a national civil defense strategy. In January 1951 the Office of Civil Defense published *Survival Under Atomic Attack*. Within a year, 20 million copies were distributed touting the main thesis that the dangers of nuclear attack were wildly exaggerated. As historian Guy Oakes has noted, "Civil Defense theorists attempted to replace this apocalyptic view of nuclear war with a very different conception designed to check American anxiety about the bomb."[15] To counter the public's fear of an atomic Armageddon, civil defense planners sought to replace the apocalyptic images of Hiroshima and Nagasaki with activities intended to ensure survival from such a blast. Not surprisingly, federal officials experimented with ways to survive a nuclear attack at the federal reservation of Los Alamos.

With Los Alamos operated by the federal government and with civil defense integral to the nation's atomic policies, the AEC funded civil defense initiatives on the Hill. The AEC did want to protect the people of Los Alamos, but it also wanted to use the community for civil defense experiments. With the AEC funds, in 1951 Los Alamos purchased new high-frequency radios and medical supplies, as well as a large number of armbands. Officials also called for volunteers to organize as neighborhood wardens. Finally, the city created a plan to protect the Hill's children.[16]

In March 1951 a disaster plan involving schoolchildren won tentative approval from the school board. In a front-page story, the *Los Alamos Herald* announced the new policy for the schools:

> If the "yellow" alert changed to the "red," room monitors would
> quickly open the windows and drop the blinds to block flying glass. All
> children would put on any available extra clothing, then file out of
> their rooms into the "structurally strongest" portions of the building
> and lie on the floor, eyes shielded in the crook of the elbow until an
> "all-clear" signal sounds.[17]

With this policy in place, school board members and parents possibly felt more confident about their children's security in the event of an atomic blast. By implementing a lie down and cover policy, civil defense officials sought to protect children from the flying debris after an explosion, but this strategy did nothing to address the health hazards from the released radioactivity. In truth, for people near ground zero, little could be done. Thus, to garner public support for the nuclear weapons program, personal safety often code switched with national security.

To experiment with civil defense strategies at Los Alamos, mock evacuations were held in November 1952. Residents drove away from their homes and offices but did not leave the Hill. This evacuation occurred right after the United States detonated its first hydrogen bomb in the South Pacific, a thermonuclear device a thousand times more powerful than the weapon that destroyed Hiroshima.[18] As one of the first community evacuations in the country, Los Alamos blazed the trail for community-wide evacuations in the rest of the country. A national program of civil defense drills began two years later in 1954, and by 1955 communities across the country were participating in coordinated evacuations. Thus, Los Alamos conducted a community-wide evacuation exercise three years before most of the rest of the nation.

The national civil defense campaign in the early 1950s included core components of education and public relations. The FCDA initiated its "Alert America" campaign in June 1951. Three caravans of ten trucks each crisscrossed the country carrying exhibits that depicted the effects of an atomic attack on the United States. The Alert America convoys were visited by 1.1 million people in 1952. Operation Alert grew out of Alert America. In 1954, after months of planning, Operation Alert staged mock atomic attacks on numerous U.S. cities to test civil defense preparedness. After each exercise the FCDA issued an estimate of casualties. For example, in Operation Alert 1956, over 8 million people died from the simulated attack, over 6 million were injured, and 24 million became homeless.[19]

A primary concern of national civil defense efforts focused on protecting students during an atomic attack. In Los Alamos officials prepared both students and parents for a possible nuclear attack. Going beyond the red and yellow alert system of 1951, the school's operating procedures for 1953 offered two plans in case of a "disaster." Plan A was contingent on an early warning of an impending disaster. If such a warning arrived in time, students were to be sent directly home and then evacuated off the Hill by their parents. Plan B addressed the possibility that "the warning received indicated insufficient time . . . for evacuation." Under Plan B teachers would instruct students to move all desks to the outside wall of the room, collect all available clothing in the room for cover and protection, climb under the desks, drape themselves with the clothing, and cover their heads with their arms. Students were to remain ducked and covered under their desks until the "all clear" signal was heard.[20] Although a nuclear attack was not mentioned as a possible disaster, Plan B could only have had that scenario in mind.

In January 1956 the schools sent home written instructions to parents outlining the procedures both students and parents should follow in an upcoming test evacuation of Los Alamos. This first community-wide test evacuation of children from the schools there tested Plan A whereby students were to go home when the alarm was sounded. The exact date and time of the test, unannounced beforehand, ended up being 2:40 P.M. on January 19, 1956, when sirens wailed an alert. Students ran home, and even the larger elementary schools cleared out within five minutes. Some high school students took the test less seriously, as they ignored the instructions to go directly to their homes and instead "went to nearby stores for their usual after-school refreshments."[21] After the students left the classrooms and supposedly went home, the test was over.

Beginning with the test evacuation of the schools in January, the year 1956 was an active period for civil defense preparedness. On May 1 a test evacuation surprised Hill residents. A first-alert siren sounded at 1:13 P.M., followed by a red alert warning at 2 P.M. In accordance with Plan A of the school's operating procedures, students were quickly sent home, and residents supposedly drove to staging areas eight miles from Los Alamos. The *New Mexican* noted that the test "was marred only by the lack of resident interest, estimated at less than sixty percent of the total population."[22] The *Albuquerque Journal* reported: "The test in general went off well with the exception of a few expected traffic jams and the locked gate at the exit of Guaje Road."[23] Perhaps those residents who did not participate in the evacuation felt immune because of the community's distance from the coasts, or perhaps they declined to join because they suspected that evacuations were futile at a time of thermonuclear explosions. Perhaps they just realized that with only two exits off the Hill, evacuations would be stalled by traffic jams. A later newspaper account acknowledged that "based on the experience of the community evacuation of last May 1, there would be 2,600 casualties, who, due to failure to participate, would be caught within the area of total destruction."[24] This estimate of casualties equaled about 15 percent of the community's population. The article did not speculate on how the rest of nonparticipating residents would survive the atomic blast.

Several federal civil defense officials observed the Los Alamos test in preparation for the national Operation Alert to be held in July. James D. Maddy, director of civilian defense for Los Alamos, stated, "The information and observations recorded during the third community evacuation held on May 1 of this year will be used as feeder material for forwarding to Civil Defense orga-

2.3 In 1955 civil defense officials on the Hill evacuated elementary schoolchildren in prepara-tion for a community evacuation. Courtesy, *Los Alamos Historical Museum Photo Archives.*

nizations at state, regional, and national levels."[25] Thus, once again Los Alamos was used as a test case for the nationwide Operation Alert drills two months later.

With all these civil defense exercises, did officials at Los Alamos enact feasible strategies for defending oneself against a nuclear attack? To be sure, civil defense precautions, like quick evacuations away from a target area and duck-and-cover drills, might have helped in the case of an attack by an atomic bomb such as the one used against Hiroshima. But with the increased strength of hydrogen bombs, such measures were no longer effective. Because they worked at one of the few towns in America where the true destructiveness of nuclear weapons was minutely studied, officials at the Los Alamos laboratory knew this. Civil defense was a response to a grim reality, but after the Soviets detonated their hydrogen bomb in November 1955, the drills acted more like a placebo, given to citizens in a target area to help them deal with their fears. Like the Los Alamos suburbs, civil defense drills gave residents a sense of secu-rity and replaced atomic anxiety with a sense of normalcy. After November

2.4 A 1955 Civil Defense exercise in which residents evacuated Los Alamos served as a model for nationwide community evacuations. Courtesy, Los Alamos Historical Museum Photo Archives.

1955, U.S. civil defense plans like duck-and-cover drills and community evacuations became inadequate to protect people from weapons a thousand times more powerful than the earlier bombs. Indeed, short of dispersing urban America to the country or moving it underground, little could be done to truly protect the nation's population against thermonuclear weapons.

Such was hinted at in 1954 in an exchange reported in newspapers between two scientists. Dr. Ralph Lapp warned that radioactive hazards from a hydrogen bomb "might persist for nine months" and that "at a distance of 110 miles from the March 1, 1954, H-bomb test, a man could have been killed three times over if he stayed in shelter only two days."[26] Atomic Energy Commission member Willard F. Libby conceded that "at 110 miles from the March 1 explosion a man could not have emerged from the shelter even for short periods during the first week."[27] Faced with the increased destructive power of thermonuclear weapons, even Winston Churchill responded with concern:

> There is an immense gulf between the atomic and the hydrogen bomb.
> The atomic bomb . . . did not carry us outside the scope of human

control or manageable events in thought or action, in peace or war. But [with the hydrogen bomb,] the entire foundation of human affairs was revolutionized, and mankind placed in a situation both measureless and laden with doom.[28]

Civil defense planning to protect against hydrogen bombs did not ensure survival. As Guy Oakes observed, "The Cold War conception of nuclear reality represented an attempt to think about the unthinkable, to conceptualize an unintelligible event and rationalize a world that seemed to be irrational, by reducing the apparently unimaginable experience of nuclear war to a set of routines."[29] Some of these routines, like community-wide evacuations, were tested in the civil defense experiments at Los Alamos.

Avoiding a real debate about the actual dangers of a nuclear attack seemed to be a goal, at least at times, of the Federal Civil Defense Administration. In the 1957 version of Operation Alert, civil defense authorities estimated that a 60 kiloton hydrogen bomb dropped on Los Alamos would kill only 153 people. Another example of avoidance of telling the public the truth about thermo-nuclear explosions came in a trucking industry publication that reprinted a statement by hydrogen bomb cocreator Dr. Edward Teller. Teller assured the public that after a full-scale attack with hydrogen weapons, "We can be back in business within a few hours."[30] Similar misrepresentations were seen in a civil defense film in which a family calmly retreated to their basement to seek shelter from an imminent attack. After the explosion rattled their shelter, the father calmly decided that the danger had passed and that they should go up and see what had happened.[31] The Los Alamos personnel who surveyed the destruction of Hiroshima and Nagasaki and who attended the test shots in the Pacific and at the Nevada Test Site (including Dr. Teller) knew the lethal effects lasted more than just a couple of hours or even days after an attack.

A more realistic evaluation of the effects of a nuclear attack was offered in May 1958. Los Alamos civil defense director James Maddy told a journalist: "Residents are urged to consider their individual capability to care for themselves and their families, should the real attack ever come. Food, clothing, medical attention and supplies would be difficult to obtain, if available at all. It might be necessary to live under very trying conditions for weeks, and even months."[32] Six years after the first hydrogen bomb exploded and multiplied the destructiveness of nuclear weapons, civil defense strategy started to accommodate the new thermonuclear reality.

Operation Alert exercises at Los Alamos continued in 1958. On May 6, "[T]his atomic city was blasted to oblivion in [a] simulated bomb attack, and a thirty-eight-mile wide strip of surrounding countryside was killed off by the severe fallout, resulting from the three megaton surface burst."[33] Residents left the city, and in a real attack they would have driven to six towns in northern New Mexico and southern Colorado—the closest over 100 miles away. The simulated fallout gave Santa Fe "a full lethal dose," and within six hours the fallout cloud had extended to Oklahoma City.[34]

With these more realistic estimates concerning the lethal impact of hydrogen bombs, civil defense officials turned to underground shelters for protection. By the mid-1960s Los Alamos had adapted forty buildings with underground facilities to accommodate its 17,000 residents in case of an attack. Maps showing the nearest shelter were part of the "welcome package" for newcomers. On the national level, communities and individuals began digging underground bomb shelters for protection.

The community of Los Alamos invented the Atomic Age and then helped create a culture for that age during the early postwar period. Touted as an atomic utopia, it offered a promise of better living though scientific endeavors to counter the terrifying prospect of the city-destroying capabilities of a nuclear weapon. As the nation's attention turned to Los Alamos to gaze into the crystal ball of the Cold War, it saw confident scientists living in modern suburbs. The storm clouds of an atomic war faded from the public's attention with such code switching.

The strategies for civil defense changed in the 1950s based on new knowledge about atomic weapons and on the introduction of the hydrogen bomb into the arsenals of the United States and the Soviet Union. This knowledge came from the scientists at Los Alamos who studied the results of the nuclear testing in the South Pacific and at the Nevada Test Site. The new community civil defense strategies also came from Los Alamos as the FCDA conducted experiments on the Hill. School and residential evacuations allowed FCDA officials to develop strategies later used in Operation Alert.

Los Alamos's impact on scientific and technological advances since 1940 is obvious. As an outpost on the Cold War frontier, it also influenced the cultural history of the 1940s and 1950s and helped mold the public's opinion about the contested nature of nuclear weapons. Atomic culture, at times forged on the anvil of Los Alamos, sought to allay Americans' atomic fears so the public would support a nuclear weapons program. By transposing the atomic utopia of the residential community of Los Alamos over nuclear weapons laboratories, the AEC effectively code switched the public's perception of such weapons.

NOTES

1. Quoted in Ferenc Szasz, *The Day the Sun Rose Twice: The Story of the Trinity Site Nuclear Explosion, July 16, 1945* (Albuquerque: University of New Mexico Press, 1984), 89.

2. Lillian Hoddeson, Paul W. Henricksen, Roger A. Meade, and Catherine Westfall, *Critical Assembly: A Technical History of Los Alamos During the Oppenheimer Years, 1943–1945* (Cambridge: Cambridge University Press, 1993), 13–14.

3. Paul Boyer, *By the Bomb's Early Light: American Thought and Culture at the Dawn of the Atomic Age* (New York: Pantheon, 1985), 122.

4. In the early Cold War period the *Denver Post,* the *Saturday Evening Post,* the *Christian Science Monitor, Life,* the *New Republic,* and the *New Yorker* all ran stories about Los Alamos.

5. Hank Trewhitt, "What Happens When Bomb Goes Off Here?" *New Mexican,* November 3, 1949, 1.

6. Quoted in Boyer, *By the Bomb's Early Light,* 7.

7. The United States Strategic Bombing Survey, *The Effects of the Atomic Bombs on Hiroshima and Nagasaki* (Santa Fe: William Gannon, 1973), 24–25.

8. Paul P. Kennedy, "How Much Civil Defense? Most of It Is on Paper," *New York Times,* July 16, 1950, E-7.

9. *Annual Report for 1951 of the Federal Civil Defense Administration* (Washington, DC: Government Printing Office, 1952), vii; "Annual Report for 1951 of the FCDA," Publication History Files, Records, RG 397, National Archives at College Park (NACP).

10. "Civil Defense Heads Meet at Los Alamos," *New Mexican,* January 10, 1951, 1.

11. "Evacuation Center Is Valley's System: Lack of Cash Doesn't Halt Preparations," *New Mexican,* January 12, 1951, 7.

12. Joe M. Clark, "'Lying Flat' Best Defense From 'Bomb,'" *New Mexican,* January 4, 1951, 3A.

13. Joe M. Clark, "Top Radiation Doses Unlikely in Most Raids," *New Mexican,* January 11, 1951, 7A.

14. Joe M. Clark, "Preventing Radiation Easier Than Removing It After It's There," *New Mexican,* January 9, 1951, 10.

15. Guy Oakes, *The Imaginary War: Civil Defense and American Cold War Culture* (New York: Oxford University Press, 1994), 52.

16. "Plan Protection for School Children in Event of Air Raid or Disaster," *Los Alamos Herald,* March 2, 1951, 1.

17. "Hill to Test Evacuation," *New Mexican,* November 2, 1952, 6.

18. Richard Rhodes, *Dark Sun: The Making of the Hydrogen Bomb* (New York: Simon and Schuster, 1995), 5–10.

19. Oakes, *Imaginary War,* 85–86.

20. Los Alamos Public Schools, *Los Alamos Operating Procedures, 1953–1954* (Los Alamos: Los Alamos Public Schools, 1953), 41.

21. "Hill Test Evacuation Includes School Kids," *New Mexican,* January 9, 1956, DiLuzio Clipping Files, Los Alamos Historical Museum Archives (DCF-LAHMA); "School Test Evacuation Termed Success," *New Mexican,* January 20, 1956, DCF-LAHMA.

22. *Annual Report, 1956,* Annual Report for 1956 of the FCDA, Publication History Files, Box 2, RG 397, NACP; "Hill Apathetic Toward Surprise 'Evacuation'"

New Mexican, May 2, 1956, DCF-LAHMA; "Only Locked Gate Mars Los Alamos 'Red' Alert," *Albuquerque Journal,* May 2, 1956, 16.

23. "Only Locked Gate."

24. "Los Alamos Girds for Friday Alert," *Albuquerque Journal,* July 15, 1956, 21.

25. Ibid.

26. "Lapp Reveals H-Bomb Fallout Far Worse Than Thought," *New Mexican,* June 13, 1955, 5.

27. Ibid.

28. Quoted in McGeorge Bundy, *Danger and Survival: Choices About the Bomb in the First Fifty Years* (New York: Random House, 1988), 198.

29. Oakes, *Imaginary War,* 79. Also John Newhouse, *War and Peace in the Nuclear Age* (New York: Knopf, 1989), 81. This insight about the difference between an atomic blast and a thermonuclear one in relation to effective civil defense came from Barton Hacker in a conversation at the Atomic West conference in Seattle, Washington, September 25, 1992.

30. "Bomb Spreads Death Over Espanola," *New Mexican,* July 18, 1957, 18; "A Statement by Dr. Edward Teller," in *Many Roads to Glory: The Story of Trucks and National Security* (Washington, DC: American Trucking Association, 1957), 30. This book is found at the New Mexico State Archives and Research Center in Santa Fe in the Mechem Special Reports file, "Federal Civil Defense Administration, 1957–58."

31. *Atomic Café,* director Kevin Rafferty, 1982. This documentary film includes clips from government films made in the 1950s on how to survive a nuclear attack.

32. "Los Alamos Joining Civil Defense Test," *New Mexican,* May 4, 1958, 6.

33. "Santa Fe Escapes, Los Alamos Is Gone," *New Mexican,* May 7, 1958, 1.

34. Ibid.

CHAPTER THREE

Uranium on the Cranium
Uranium Mining and Popular Culture

MICHAEL A. AMUNDSON

Since 1948, uranium has been mined in the United States first to supply the raw material for the nation's Cold War atomic defenses and then for fuel for U.S. nuclear power plants. Like most things atomic, uranium mining has been part of America's nuclear culture, and its image has changed over time. During the government-sponsored rush of the 1950s, uranium mining was all the rage and served as a sexy plot device for television shows and movies, rock and roll songs, board games, Viewmaster reels, and even the built environment.

Although most of these popular culture forms only used uranium as a vehicle to push tired themes of good guys versus bad guys, more sophisticated examples understood the significance of the government role in this boom, the importance of uranium to national defense, and the potential health hazards of radioactivity. All of them served dual purposes. On one level they reflected U.S. interest in the new industry and the tremendous potential of nuclear energy. On another level these forms were part of the country's developing disassociation with the devastating potential of nuclear warfare.

As the once-thought-to-be-rare mineral proved plentiful in the late 1950s and early 1960s and the government abandoned its flush market, the uranium industry collapsed and the 1950s miracle ore dropped out of favor. As the 1960s

reinvented America, uranium's image changed too with the increasing awareness of the effects of radiation and radon on its underground miners. By the
time nuclear power plant demands launched a second boom during the 1970s
energy crisis, uranium mining had lost its luster in the public imagination.
Instead of pop culture gimmicks, high-culture fiction, poetry, and movies depicted the long-term environmental, health, and economic effects of uranium
mining. Extracting the atomic ore had become serious business. This chapter
will explore these trends by briefly explaining the history of U.S. uranium
mining, will survey a variety of its forms in popular culture, and will then
summarize some broad themes that connect uranium mining to other forms of
atomic culture during this time.

Emerson once said that a weed is a plant whose virtues are unknown. This
phrase aptly describes the history of uranium in the United States. Primarily
found in a yellow mineral called carnotite on the Colorado Plateau, uranium
was an extremely rare metal prior to the 1950s. Before 1939, uranium was
used in the United States as a low-grade source of radium and as a chemical
dye for paints, glass, and ceramics. From 1898 to the early 1920s, less than one-
half pound of radium was extracted from 67,000 tons of carnotite on the
Colorado Plateau.[1] When richer mines in the Belgian Congo (now Demo-
cratic Republic of Congo) and Canada were put into production in the 1920s,
the U.S. market collapsed. Then in the mid-1930s it was discovered that vana-
dium, another mineral present in carnotite, was useful as a steel alloy. From
1936 to 1942 carnotite was again mined and processed at sites all over the
plateau including Uravan, Colorado, and Monticello and Blanding, Utah. The
more costly uranium and radium ores were simply discarded.[2]

The 1939 discovery that uranium could be used in a fission reaction brought
the mineral to the forefront of national security. Within a year, Albert Einstein
penned his famous letter to Franklin Roosevelt advocating the atomic bomb;
shortly thereafter the United States found itself at war. When the Army Corps
of Engineers organized the top-secret Manhattan Project to build the bomb,
the greatest sources of uranium in the world were the tailings piles of the two
richest radium mines in the Belgian Congo and Canada's Northwest Territo-
ries and the leftover tailings of carnotite on the Colorado Plateau. Only 14
percent of the Manhattan Engineer District's (MED) three atomic bombs were
derived from these domestic tailings.[3]

During the Cold War, the exploration and production of uranium became
a major component of U.S. national security. Following World War II, the newly
created Atomic Energy Commission (AEC) took over the MED's program as
all fissionable materials became the sole legal property of the federal govern-

ment. To ensure an adequate domestic uranium supply, the AEC then implemented a series of subsidies for exploration, mining, and milling of uranium for national defense. These incentives created a uranium rush to the interior West similar to the gold rushes a century before.[4]

The search for new domestic uranium deposits began in the Uravan mineral belt on the Colorado Plateau and slowly radiated outward. Aided by guaranteed prices and haulage allowances, local weekend prospectors began to spend their spare time searching the back country for uranium. To aid the amateur, popular magazines published the first articles on where to look for uranium.[5] In 1949 the AEC joined the excitement by issuing the booklet *Prospecting for Uranium*. This palm-sized handbook included chapters showing the major uranium-bearing minerals, explaining the different types of ore deposits, testing and prospecting with radiation-detecting instruments, assaying and selling procedures, explaining laws and regulations concerning mining claims, frequently asked questions, and an appendix of price schedules, sources for Geiger counters, and geological information.[6]

Prospectors in the American West soon found uranium in nearly every western state. Major strikes transformed the towns of Moab, Utah, and Grants, New Mexico, into self-proclaimed "Uranium Capitals of the World." Other mining and milling communities included Jeffrey City, Wyoming; Uravan and Durango, Colorado; Tuba City, Arizona; and Shiprock, New Mexico. In these boomtowns, local entrepreneurs held "Miss Uranium" pageants and adopted the atomic ore into the built environment with an Atomic Café and Uranium Office Building in Moab and Grants sporting a Chinese restaurant in the Uranium Café. A new penny stock market boomed in Salt Lake City as investors poured capital into the industry.[7]

During the heyday of the government's uranium procurement program, uranium became part of American popular culture. Popular magazines of the day followed the big strikes and told Americans how to outfit themselves for prospecting. The May 23, 1955, issue of *Life* magazine compared the $180 outlay for equipment for the part-time prospector (Geiger counter, canteen, and maps) versus the $3,529 needed for the well-heeled searcher—including jeep, drill hole and reel assembly, and several Geiger counters. A photo in the article even showed an all-American family outfitted in their "prospecting duds" including a girl's "diggerette jr. suit" and her mother's "U-235 suit."[8]

Movies picked up on the popularity of uranium mining. In 1950 the comedy team of Stan Laurel and Oliver Hardy starred in their final film together, titled both *Utopia* and *Atoll K*. The forced plot showed a very aged duo inheriting an island in the Pacific. Once there, they discover that their island contains uranium, and a huge boom follows, destroying their peace and quiet. Interestingly, this Hollywood version of the boomtown rush actually preceded the major uranium booms in Grants, Moab, and other western towns. As unlikely as it is to think of Stan and Ollie involved in a uranium boom, another 1950 film that used uranium in its plot offers just as unusual a cast of characters. In the Roy Rogers classic *Bells of Coronado,* Rogers took on the unlikely role of an undercover insurance investigator following a mysterious murderer plotting to sell uranium to a foreign power. With the help of Dale Evans and Pat Brady and utilizing jeeps, airplanes, and, of course, Trigger—the "smartest horse in the movies"—Rogers captured the murderer and saved the country. *Bells of Coronado* clearly addresses the national security angle of the uranium story, invoking the Atomic Energy Act of 1946 that made it illegal to sell uranium to anyone but the U.S. government.[9]

The cowboy image resurfaced in another uranium film later that decade. In 1955 Leo Gorcey, Huntz Hall, and the Bowery Boys starred in *Dig That Uranium.* A lobby card for *Dig That Uranium* shows two cowboys, bearing six-shooters and dressed in Nashville garb, protecting a sparsely dressed woman in some sort of mine. Another poster has one of the men holding his Geiger counter over the same woman with the caption "And BOY, how their [G]eiger counters click when they meet those babes from the Badlands."[10]

The 1956 Columbia Pictures film *Uranium Boom,* starring Dennis Morgan and Patricia Medina, focused on the prospecting rush and its effect on western boomtowns. A poster for *Uranium Boom* shows another buxom brunette and two prospectors holding Geiger counters with the phrase "The inside story of the atom-age boomtowns!" Another scene on the poster, also shown in detail in a lobby card, shows a group of ax and pick-wielding prospectors swinging their tools and pushing and shoving. It's not clear whether they are digging for uranium or are involved in a big fight.[11]

Placing big stars in bad plots did not help the uranium-themed films. In 1953 John Huston directed *Beat the Devil* starring Humphrey Bogart, Peter Lorre, and Gina Lollobrigida. In this convoluted caper spoof of classics *The Maltese Falcon* and *Key Largo,* Bogart and Lorre were part of a gang going to British East Africa in search of uranium. Beyond the use of uranium as a prop, the film rarely mentions it. Bogart's forgettable character properly summarized the film in its introduction. Describing his gang, Bogart said, "These were my associates in a quest for uranium, an element that not one of them knew anything about except that you could get dough from it—big dough." Another African-based uranium film was the forgettable, low-budget Italian film *Desert Detour* starring Omar Sharif.[12]

3.1 Dig That Uranium poster, c. 1957. Michael Amundson collection.

Perhaps the most famous uranium film actually spoofed both uranium mining and nuclear testing. *The Atomic Kid* (1954), written by Blake Edwards, starred Mickey Rooney and Robert Strauss as uranium prospectors wandering the

Nevada desert looking for hot rocks. Along the way they stumbled into what appears to be a deserted town. What they actually found, however, was DOOM TOWN, the Atomic Energy Commission testing grounds! And if that's not enough, they were there just as the AEC detonated an atomic device. Somehow surviving the blast while at ground zero, Rooney began to glow before realizing the marketability of being the first human being to survive an atomic bomb—somehow forgetting the many survivors of Hiroshima and Nagasaki.[13]

Animated cartoons about uranium mining showed the prevalence of the boom in popular culture. In 1956 a Terrytoons short called *Uranium Fever* depicted a scruffy western miner who gave up his trusted old burro named Geranium (what else could rhyme with uranium) for a jeep to prospect for atomic ore. When the jeep failed, the miner was tossed over a cliff where he caught on to a branch, Beetle Bailey style. He was then attacked by vultures pecking at him in a Promethean fashion, as if the gods were angry that the prospectors had given mankind nuclear fire. After he was saved by his trusty burro, the message is clear: trusted friends will beat technology every time. In the 1960 Popeye cartoon called *Uranium on the Cranium,* Popeye and Olive Oyl were on a desert island in search of uranium. After discovering the glowing ore, they were attacked by Brutus in an ape suit. While Olive Oyl was tied to a rock, a real gorilla beat up Popeye and threw him through a tree, knocking him useless as Brutus started to mine uranium. With the help of a little spinach (his own uranium?), Popeye avenged Brutus and the ape, saved Olive Oyl, and made the rightful claim to the uranium.[14]

A few common threads emerge among the movies. Although these films portrayed various aspects of the uranium industry including the worldwide search, boomtown rushes, national security interests, the government monopsony market, and western settings, these points did not offset their problems. Several of the movies interwove nuclear testing and uranium prospecting to the point of confusion. Although both were happening in the American West in the 1950s, there were very few examples of such mix-ups. In spring of 1953 the Grants, New Mexico, newspaper reported that the entire town was sitting on a hot uranium mine. Geiger counters were soon buzzing all over town. Everybody thought they were going to get rich until a Los Alamos engineer reported the next week that they had, in fact, not discovered uranium but been hit by fallout from a test upwind in Nevada. The town was disappointed.[15]

To conclude, these uranium films used contrived plots with pre-Atomic Age actors and uranium gimmicks in a rapidly changing nuclear age. Roy Rogers, Stan and Ollie, and Mickey Rooney just do not belong in films dealing with atomic issues.

Post–World War II television offered no better uranium spin. Again using pre–World War II stars in postwar stories, a number of 1950s television shows also used the uranium rush to sell their plots. In the 1950s the *Amos and Andy* show featured a uranium storyline where the Kingfish plotted to sell Amos some swampland that was supposed to be a uranium mine. Once again, atomic props such as Geiger counters and heavily packed mules were the order of the day. Even Lucy and Desi got into the act. In the January 3, 1958, airing of the *Lucy and Desi Comedy Hour*—a sixty-minute sequel to their famous show— Lucy, Desi, Fred, Ethel, and guest star Fred MacMurray joined in a big uranium hunt. The plot went something like this. While performing in Las Vegas, Ricky forbids Lucy to join in the rush and go uranium hunting. Not to be outdone, Lucy creates a fake newspaper with a headline that reads "Big Uranium Strike Outside Las Vegas." When a hotel cleaning lady finds the paper, uranium fever strikes the gang, and they go off in search of uranium. Accidentally dropping a radioactive sample designed to test their Geiger counter, they go crazy when they hear a buzz and get into a big race against Fred MacMurray to see who can get back to Las Vegas first and stake their million-dollar claim.[16]

Like Hollywood, television offered a few pieces of truth amid much screwball comedy. Although Amos and Andy certainly presented a racist view of African Americans, the fact is that a few African Americans were involved in the uranium rush. One story from *Ebony* described the only black prospector in Moab, Utah, in the 1950s. As for Lucy, although Las Vegas offered a nice setting for Ricky and a big bonus was paid for new high-grade uranium discoveries, little actual uranium prospecting occurred in that area.

Scholars have shown how early rock and roll featured atomic themes, and uranium mining was no exception.[17] In 1957 the Commodores recorded an Artie Glenn do-wop song called "Uranium." The lyrics started with the catchy syncopation of "U-ranium, U-ranium." They then decried oil and gold extraction before drawing on typical stories of packing mules to prospect for uranium. Two years later Warren Smith's 1957 rockabilly song "Uranium Rock" included a driving beat and forgettable lyrics that also made allusions to Geiger counters and instant wealth.[18]

Companies also used the uranium boom to sell toys and games. A 1957 Viewmaster reel featured Roy Rogers in "Uranium Fever." This story—probably created especially for the seven-scene Viewmaster—again featured Roy, Dale, and Pat Brady using Trigger, Nellybell the jeep, and a helicopter to track down and capture uranium claim jumpers. About the same time, Ny-Lint manufactured a toy truck called the "Uranium Hauler." This green dump truck looked like an army truck of some kind, with stars and stripes on the body. Despite the

3.2 Nylint's 1950s uranium hauler toy truck. Michael Amundson collection.

fact that the government did not mine uranium, the truck featured a hydraulic dumping bed, and one can just imagine some kid playing with the truck and pretending he is mining uranium for America's national security. Games companies also marketed uranium board games to provide family fun. A very simple game called "Uranium" featured a dial that players spun and then trekked their way across the board toward uranium.[19]

A much more sophisticated game was the 1950s Gardner Games electronic board game called "Uranium Rush." Although somewhat goofy in its own right, this game featured the most lifelike aspects of the real uranium boom including scenery, the government's role, and capital investment. The board was colored to look like a variety of western landscapes including "purple mountains," "green hill country," and "sandy desert." Each player was grubstaked with $15,000, and play proceeded by spinning an arrow that directed the player toward the proper landscape for prospecting. As each mine was staked, the player had to decide whether to sell the claim to another or "develop" it. If the player chose the latter, the player paid the government bank $1,000 and took an electronic "Geiger counter"—a small flashlight-like object—and held it to the electronic game board. If the Geiger counter's light flashed, the player had discovered uranium and received $50,000 from the government bank.[20]

After testing the claim, the player picked one of thirty "government cards" from the deck and followed its instructions. These cards included gags such as bills for new Geiger counters, hospital fees for treatment after mountain lion attacks, and rewards for finding oil, silver, gold, and copper prospects. Others

3.3 Uranium Rush board game box top. Michael Amundson collection.

were more attuned to Cold War attitudes. One card ordered the Geiger counter to be skipped past the next player in case he or she might be an enemy agent. Another provided the lucky player with an extra $5,000 because the government bought the claim for an air force base, and another awarded the player an extra $20,000 for discovering extra–high-grade uranium ore. One card forced the player to pay the bank $10,000 to clear title for the last claim because the ground was owned by an "Indian Tribe." The prospector with the most money when all claims had been staked won the game.[21]

Although "Uranium Rush" was only one of many such toys during this time, it serves as an important symbol of uranium's transformation in the early days of the Cold War. Although the Manhattan Project had been top secret, the 1950s uranium boom was a much advertised and very popular public program. In fact, the seeming randomness of spinning a dial and selecting a card seemed to mirror the image that anyone could—with a little luck—discover uranium, preserve national security, and become a millionaire in the process. This could be done in a variety of western landscapes including mountains, deserts, hill country, and even Indian reservations. At the same time, the use of "government cards" suggested that Uncle Sam would regulate the whole affair and maintain security by being wary of "enemy agents."

Although not to the same degree or complexity, parts of this same story had been told in many movies and television shows. While Mickey Rooney, Stan and Ollie, and Lucy and the gang were trying to get rich quick, Roy Rogers was making sure claim jumpers did not prevail and that mysterious murderers did not sell uranium to foreign spies. All of these popular culture examples generally got the setting right—the American West—although too many confused nuclear testing in the South Pacific or Nevada with uranium prospecting in the Rocky Mountain West.

On a deeper level, the creation and popularity of "Uranium Rush" and similar Cold War toys represent the subordination of national security for the humor of popular culture. The possibilities of instant wealth and notoriety seemed to replace the guardedness of national security thought needed during the Manhattan Project. Although the veil of nuclear secrecy had been lifted and the effects of atomic bombs on the Japanese well documented, the American public separated the horrors of the atom bomb from the romance of another fabled American mineral rush.

The popular culture images carry this theme. The "Uranium Rush" box top shows a young prospector leading a mule but carrying what looks like an atomic bomb or missile. The cover photo for "Lucy Hunts Uranium" shows the gang with Geiger counters and surprised, goofy looks on their faces. Or who can ever forget the great scene on the *Dig That Uranium* poster showing a man running a Geiger counter over the exposed leg of a beautiful woman and the line about "those babes from the Badlands."

The Manhattan Project's famed "compartmentalization" had seemingly been publicly replaced by a sort of accommodation in which Americans joked about parts of atomic technology while repressing others. Patriotism and national security were rarely discussed; Geiger counters, radioactivity, "glowing in the dark," and getting rich quick were the rage. There was little thought of the final use of all this uranium. A 1946 poll revealed that 47 percent of Americans were not worried or worried very little about the atomic bomb. Instead, people trusted science, the government, and God to protect them or suggested that such worry was useless.[22] Thus, as the Atomic Energy Commission created and subsidized a massive search for uranium to use in atomic bombs to protect national security, the American public trusted its leaders and made the uranium boom another Old West gold rush adventure.[23] The resulting mix of popular magazines, bad movies, goofy television shows, rock and roll songs, Viewmaster reels, toy trucks, and board games represented an American public both at home with things atomic and at the same time repressing their very purpose.

By 1958 the government's uranium stockpile had grown so large that the AEC decreased its subsidies, placed embargoes against importation of foreign sources, and established allocations on existing domestic sources to sustain the now dependent industry until private nuclear-powered utilities came needing uranium. The uranium prospecting boom collapsed, and the industry began a dozen-year decline.[24] As the 1960s cultural revolution, the Vietnam War, and many social movements changed America, uranium also underwent a transformation as scientists and doctors finally began to publicize the effects of fallout and radiation from years of atomic testing, as well as the hazards of radon gas and radioactivity on uranium miners. When uranium "resurfaced" as a competitive energy source during the fossil fuel crisis of the 1970s, it no longer held the sex appeal it had in the 1950s. Instead, uranium's environmental, health, and economic effects were included in fiction, poetry, and film—almost presaging the change all atomic culture endured after Three Mile Island. Uranium was already part of the problem in high-culture accounts of the early 1970s. Never as popular as it had been during the 1950s, the few examples of uranium mining in American culture focused on its inherent dangers.[25]

The best-known writers to focus on uranium's shift from gimmick to hazard were Native American writers in the Southwest. Both N. Scott Momaday's Pulitzer Prize–winning *House Made of Dawn* (1968) and Leslie Marmon Silko's *Ceremony* (1977) included discussions of the environmental and cultural effects of uranium mining on the pueblo peoples of the Southwest. Movie director Michael Apted used similar themes, this time set on the Sioux lands of South Dakota, in the 1992 film *Thunderheart*. In each of these cases, uranium mining has ruined the sacred environment and endangered a generation of miners while providing them with little economic gain amid growing cultural debate.[26]

Popular writer Edward Abbey used uranium as an antagonist in his fiction. After serving as a park ranger at Moab's Arches National Monument during the end of the first uranium boom, Abbey decried the boom's effects briefly in his 1968 classic *Desert Solitaire*. Although the atomic ore was mostly left out of *The Monkey Wrench Gang,* Abbey capitalized on the second boom as the culprit in its posthumously published 1990 sequel *Hayduke Lives!*[27] In this story the Gang's foe, Bishop J. Dudley Love, is building a large uranium mine in southern Utah that becomes the Gang's focus of attention. At the opening ceremonies, Abbey makes Bishop Love the spokesman for the uranium industry and its efforts to refute the environmentalists:

Uranium is poison, they say. Well, I want to tell you folks something different: that uranium smells like money to me. [Cheers.] It smells like jobs to me. [More cheers!] Hundreds of jobs right here in Hardrock and Landfill County and just across the line in northern Arizona. Hundreds? I mean thousands of jobs. . . . Poison they say? Cancer? Leukemia? Listen, folks, I'm here to tell you there's one man don't fear the smell of uranium, don't fear the smell of radon. Because I lived here all my life and I worked in the first uranium mines and I'm still here and I don't glow in the dark—[laughter] and by all heck and tarnation I'm happy as a hog in heaven.[28]

Bishop Love then reached inside his suit coat and removed a small chunk of carnotite—"a friable, yellowish, highly radioactive uranium ore—from an inside pocket." He continued:

That's carnotite, folks. That's what we got south of here in those big canyons off the Grand Canyon. Now you know and I know the uranium industry is in a slump these days, the American nuclear business is shot to hell, the doggone environmentalists are shutting down the nuke plants, this ore is so rich, my friends, such high grade ore, that even with yellowcake down to seventeen dollars a pound this stuff is worth mining. Let the price go down to ten a pound, this carnotite will still pay. Europe wants it if we don't. And Japan, Brazil, them places. This is pay dirt, men. Radioactive gold.[29]

Love checked the ore with a Geiger counter and ate it! He concluded, "Radiation is good for you. Uranium is good for you! Uranium is good for Utah and Arizona! The uranium industry is good for America!" Like the original, the rest of the book features outlandish escapades before the Monkey Wrench Gang finally outwits Bishop Love and stops uranium mining once and for all.[30]

Perhaps the most insightful account of uranium mining's new role in American culture is found in the poems of Acoma Indian poet Simon Ortiz. Having seen his people's lands torn up by the 1950s boom and the subsequent economic and health effects of decades of uranium mining on his people, Ortiz contextualizes problems of both boom and bust. In "It Was That Indian," Ortiz describes nearby Grants, New Mexico, during both the boomtown problems of the 1950s and the later bust. Focusing on Paddy Martinez, the Navajo who made the initial 1950 strike, Ortiz finds uranium to be just another way Anglo society can blame Native peoples. Ortiz spends the first half of the poem on a litany of boomtown problems that were blamed on Martinez. Hardly the "Uranium Capital of the World" it ascribed itself to be, Ortiz's Grants then blames Martinez for all the health problems later blamed on uranium mining. Thus, whether boomtown problems or economic bust and health problems, the Native peoples of the region once again get the blame.[31] Other Ortiz poems

3.4 Toxic waste car, Lionel, c. 1995. Michael Amundson collection.

suggest that Acoma and Laguna Pueblo men who worked in the mines were used as strike breakers and had limited upward mobility. Like Momaday, Silko, and Abbey, Ortiz paints uranium mining as an antagonist, gobbling up the environment and spewing deadly gases and radiation on its defenseless peoples.[32]

By the mid-1990s uranium culture had come full circle as a new generation seemingly reminisced about the boom days of the 1950s. In 1997 Lionel, the model railroad company, introduced its "Toxic Waste Car." Complete with its "uranium waste load," the flatbed car featured two small white pylons with radiation symbols, the letters "AEC" ensconced by a nuclear symbol, and the words "DANGER URANIUM." On top, red lights blinked as the car circled the track. The instructions read:

> Congratulations! Your Lionel railroad has won the government contract
> to safely remove toxic waste from your friendly local nuclear power
> plant for transport to remote dump sites located all across the conti-
> nent. The simulated toxic waste load is held in two containers from
> which an ominously radiating light flashes on and off whenever the
> track is energized.[33]

With its reference to the "friendly" local nuke plant, the need for "remote" dump sites, and the clear note that only "simulated" toxic waste was included, the "Toxic Waste Car" seemed to suggest that American atomic culture had indeed completed the nuclear fuel cycle, as children today could apparently remove the spent uranium from their parents' toy power plants and take it somewhere else. At the same time, the fact that nuclear waste was now a toy to be played with seemed reminiscent of the uranium hauler from four decades previous. From pop icon to public enemy to something in between, uranium mining continues to be a part of American culture. Given uranium's extended half life, Americans will no doubt have "uranium on the cranium" for years to come.

NOTES

1. William L. Chenoweth, "The Uranium-Vanadium Deposits of the Uravan Mineral Belt and Adjacent Areas, Colorado and Utah," *New Mexico Geological Society Guidebook,* 32nd Field Conference, Western Slope, Colorado, 1981.

2. Michael A. Amundson, *Yellowcake Towns: Uranium Mining Communities in the American West* (Boulder: University Press of Colorado, 2002), 1–15.

3. Ibid., 17–35.

4. Ibid., 17–36.

5. "How to Hunt for Uranium," *Popular Science* (February 1946): 121–123; "How to Find Uranium," *Time,* April 21, 1947, 86; "Out Where the Click Is Louder," *Time,* July 18, 1949, 53.

6. United States Atomic Energy Commission and United States Geological Survey, *Prospecting for Uranium* (Washington, DC: Government Printing Office, 1949, revised 1951).

7. Amundson, *Yellowcake Towns,* 28. Photos showing an atomic pageant appear on p. 84, and examples of the built environment can be found in photos on 63, 64, 94, and 122,

8. Andreas Feininger, "History's Greatest Metal Hunt," *Life,* May 23, 1955, 25–35.

9. *Utopia,* dir. Leo Joannon, 1950; *Bells of Coronado,* Republic Pictures Corporation, 1950.

10. *Dig That Uranium,* prod. Ben Schwalb, 1955.

11. *Uranium Boom,* prod. Sam Katzman, 1956.

12. *Beat the Devil,* dir. John Huston, 1953; *Desert Detour,* dir. Richard Potter, 1957.

13. *The Atomic Kid,* dir. Leslie H. Martinson, 1954. Nuclear testing is discussed in A. Constadina Titus, *Bombs in the Backyard: Atomic Testing and American Politics,* 2nd ed. (Reno: University of Nevada Press, 2001).

14. *Uranium Fever,* Terrytunes, 1956; *Uranium on the Cranium,* dir. Paul Fennell, 1960.

15. "Geiger Counters Act Haywire," Grants *Beacon,* April 23, 1953.

16. *The Amos and Andy Show,* "Uranium Mine," circa 1957; *The Lucy and Desi Comedy Hour,* "Lucy Hunts Uranium," January 3, 1958.

17. Allan M. Winkler, *Life Under A Cloud: American Anxiety About the Atom* (Urbana: University of Illinois Press, 1999).

18. The Commodores, "Uranium," circa 1957; Warren Smith, "Uranium Rock," circa 1957.

19. *The Roy Rogers Show,* "Uranium Fever," 1956; Ny-Lint Toys, "Uranium Hauler," circa 1955; Howard Boughner, *Uranium: A Game for Two to Four "Prospectors"* (Akron, OH: Saalfield, 1955).

20. Gardner Games, "Uranium Rush," circa 1957.

21. Issues regarding uranium mining on Native American reservations are explained in Peter Eichstaedt, *If You Poison Us: Uranium and Native Americans* (Santa Fe: Red Crane, 1994).

22. Leonard S. Cottrell Jr. and Syliva Eberhart, *American Opinion on World Affairs in the Atomic Age* (Princeton: Princeton University Press, 1948), 108–111. Discussion of this poll and its revelation is found in Spencer R. Weart, *Nuclear Fear: A History of Images* (Cambridge: Harvard University Press, 1988), 134.

23. This attitude is expressed in Kevin Rafferty, Jayne Loader, and Pierce Rafferty's classic Cold War documentary, *Atomic Café,* 1982.

24. Amundson, *Yellowcake Towns,* 105–114.

25. Ibid., 115–172; Winkler, *Life Under a Cloud,* 165–208; Titus, *Bombs in the Backyard,* 114–130.

26. N. Scott Momaday, *House Made of Dawn* (New York: Harper and Row, 1968); Leslie Marmon Silko, *Ceremony* (New York: Viking, 1977); *Thunderheart,* dir. Michael Apted, Columbia TriStar Home Video, circa 1992.

27. Edward Abbey, *Desert Solitaire: A Season in the Wilderness* (New York: McGraw Hill, 1968); *The Monkey Wrench Gang* (Philadelphia: Lippincott, 1975); *Hayduke Lives! A Novel* (Boston: Little, Brown, 1990).

28. Abbey, *Hayduke Lives,* 22–24.

29. Ibid.

30. Ibid., 23.

31. Simon Ortiz, *Woven Stone* (Tucson: University of Arizona Press, 1992), 293–334.

32. Ibid.

33. "Toxic Waste Car," #71-6666-250 (5/97), Lionel LLC, 1997.

Confronting the "Capitalist Bomb"

The Neutron Bomb and American Culture

Scott C. Zeman

"People in the United States and everywhere else in the free world are being frightened by the specter of a new doomsday weapon . . . a death-ray weapon which would kill human beings without damaging property."[1] So wrote famed science reporter William Laurence in the May 5, 1962, issue of *Saturday Evening Post*. The "death-ray weapon" to which Laurence referred was the neutron bomb, and it was more than mere specter. That same year American scientists and engineers had successfully tested a neutron device in the Nevada desert.

Described at the time as a "radically new" weapon design, the neutron bomb is basically a small-yield thermonuclear device that, when detonated, emits large amounts of neutrons. This characteristic means it kills primarily by massive neutron bombardment, not by blast or heat, as is the case with conventional nuclear weapons. Because the blast effects are relatively limited, the devastation to buildings and other structures remains minimal. This property-friendly feature quickly earned it the title of the "capitalist bomb." As a tactical nuclear weapon, the neutron bomb was developed primarily for the defense of Western Europe against a Soviet attack. By penetrating Soviet tanks and armor, neutrons would kill the enemy but not leave European cities in radioactive ruins.

As we have seen in preceding chapters, U.S. concerns about "the bomb" expressed themselves in a variety of cultural forms. Thus far the historical and cultural analysis has focused mainly on reactions to atomic and thermo-nuclear weapons—the A-bomb and the H-bomb. This chapter will explore cultural concerns over the N-bomb: how Americans confronted the "capitalist bomb."

From its inception, the neutron bomb provoked controversy. In fact, two distinct public rows occurred over the neutron bomb: the first between 1959 and 1963 and a second, later reprise between 1977 and 1983. What is of par-ticular interest in examining U.S. cultural reactions to the neutron bomb is that, unlike the atomic or hydrogen bombs, concerns over the development of the neutron bomb surfaced at two different times, almost twenty years apart. Thus, by comparing reactions to the neutron bomb in two different historical-cultural contexts, one can see how American atomic culture had changed over the course of those two decades.

The first neutron bomb controversy occurred near the end of America's High Atomic Culture era (roughly 1949–1963). High Atomic Culture was characterized by a Cold War consensus, civil defense drills, fallout shelters, and lingering hopes for a bright atomic future. Some of the most vibrant expres-sions of High Atomic Culture can be found in the many science fiction films of the period that dealt with nuclear concerns. Classics like *The Day the Earth Stood Still* (1951), *This Island Earth* (1954), and *Forbidden Planet* (1956) re-flected the fears of the period, as well as a sense of awe at the atom's seemingly limitless potential. In *Forbidden Planet* thermonuclear energy had given a long-lost race of beings of the planet Altair 4, the Krel, the ability to achieve both "true creation"—a "civilization without instrumentality"—as well as the power to destroy their entire race in a single night.[2]

When the prospect of a neutron bomb first reached the public in the late 1950s, the U.S. response proved very much in keeping with the dominant tone of High Atomic Culture: awe and wonder, as well as trepidation. The neutron bomb was often referred to as an "atomic death ray," not unlike the ray guns brandished by beings from other planets or earthling space explorers, as re-flected in the science fiction of the period.

If *Forbidden Planet* represented typical concerns of High Atomic Culture, Stanley Kubric's brilliant apocalyptic comedy *Dr. Strangelove* (1964) set the tone for Late Atomic Culture.[3] Awe and fear had been eclipsed by cynicism and mind-numbing terror; death-ray guns had transmuted to doomsday ma-chines. When the neutron bomb resurfaced as a cultural concern in the late 1970s, it became emblematic of changed attitudes toward all things atomic.

This time Americans greeted it with shudders of horror and cries of immorality. The neutron bomb was the quintessential Late Atomic nightmare.

The basic concept for the neutron bomb made its way into the popular press as early as the summer of 1957. Readers who looked closely at the June 3 issue of *Time* magazine might have noticed that a short piece on the hazards associated with nuclear tests mentioned that "effort is being invested in designing bombs that create a maximum amount of short-lived radioactivity. Such weapons might depopulate whole countries without keeping the invaders from living in the silent houses after [only] a month or two."[4]

Much of the early press coverage of the neutron bomb linked it directly to the effort to produce the so-called clean bomb (i.e., a fission-free hydrogen bomb). The November 30, 1959, issue of *Time* explained that "after ten years of secret planning, the U.S. is on the verge of developing a true 'clean bomb' . . . the neutron bomb." Such a device would fire "millions of fatal, invisible" neutrons at enemy soldiers but would not damage buildings or machines, and it would leave no lingering radioactivity. The magazine further noted that the Soviet Union also had the ability to develop such devices but that the voluntary nuclear test moratorium, in place since late 1958, was hindering the United States from moving beyond the theoretical stage.[5]

In the years between 1959 and 1963, *U.S. News and World Report, Newsweek,* and *Time*—the three largest and most widely read news magazines in the United States—each carried several stories about the neutron bomb. In May 1960 *U.S. News and World Report* declared the neutron "death-ray" bomb the "most terrible bomb of all."[6] The following February a *Time* magazine piece referred not to death rays but to a weapon that rained "showers of neutron 'bullets'" down upon the enemy.[7] The April 4, 1960, issue of *Newsweek* contained a short review of an article by physicist Freeman Dyson that had recently appeared in *Foreign Affairs.*[8] In the article Dyson described the possibility of a "third generation . . . fission-free bomb" and noted that the Soviets had been doing research in this area since 1952. Dyson maintained that compared with earlier bombs, the weapon would create less radioactivity in the target zone and would offer "far greater versatility in infantry warfare." Reflecting the tone of High Atomic Culture, Dyson connected these new nuclear weapons breakthroughs to visionary hopes for the future, such as the development of atomic engines for "efficient propulsion of a space ship" and "long range and economic space travel."[9]

Popular Science and *Popular Mechanics* magazines also commented on the futuristic new weapon. *Popular Science* proclaimed the neutron bomb "a real Buck Rogers job; a true death ray" that killed people but left buildings untouched.

The magazine also linked the "neutron death ray" device to the quest for a clean bomb, one that, it speculated, would likely use TNT to initiate fusion.[10] *Popular Science* continued with a more extensive and detailed discussion in January 1962. "The eeriest weapon is the death ray," the magazine noted. "It was invented years ago by the science fiction writers. Now the off-again on-again hydrogen-bomb race is making it come true in a strange form."[11] A short piece in *Popular Mechanics* described the neutron bomb in similar fashion, noting that the "death ray, that fantastic invention of science fiction writers, someday may be a terribly real weapon for both the U.S. and the U.S.S.R."[12]

William Laurence, America's premier atomic journalist and the only reporter to witness the Trinity Test, enlightened readers about the neutron bomb in the pages of *Saturday Evening Post*. Laurence noted that the N-bomb was theoretically possible but was at least half a century away in terms of development because of the difficulties in producing a clean fusion detonation. Laurence encouraged the American people not to fear such a "fantastic weapon" and warned that the United States should not involve itself in a neutron bomb race with the Soviet Union.[13] And even if the United States could overcome the daunting challenges of making a practical neutron bomb, Laurence surmised, because of its small effective range (he estimated the maximum lethal range at one and one-quarter miles) and the relative ease with which one could use shielding as protection, military usefulness might remain limited. It would be, Laurence quipped, like "killing flies with a big-game rifle." He dismissed neutron bomb fears as unfounded, caused by "alarmists," and little more than a "disturbing nightmare in the course of other nuclear progress which, with peaceful application, may well lead to a brighter and fuller future for all humanity."[14]

Although the neutron bomb received a good deal of coverage in *Time, Newsweek,* and *Popular Science* from 1959 through 1963, it received relatively scant attention in contemporary music, literature, and film. This absence seems to indicate that the neutron bomb did not permeate American popular culture in the same way it would two decades later. However, the neutron bomb did find its way into a few foreign films. The British film *The Poisoned Earth* (1961) centers on a small town situated next to a site where development of a "neutron-type bomb" is taking place. The situation ultimately provokes a clash between protestors and residents.[15] In a less serious vein, the Mexican *Neutron the Masked Wrestler* trilogy features the superhero wrestler, Neutron, foiling the attempts of villains bent on acquiring the neutron bomb for evil purposes. In *Neutron el Enmascardo Negro* (*Neutron and the Black Mask,* 1961), Neutron battles scientists who have visions of world domination. In the second film in the trilogy, *Los Automatas de la Muerte* (*Neutron v. the Robots of Death,* 1962), the masked hero

The
Death-Ray
Bomb

Detonators of
shaped TNT

Deuterium gas
(liberated from
lithium compound)

Fuse timed to
burst high
above ground

4.1 The "Death-Ray Bomb" from Popular Science, August 1960.

fights the sinister Dr. Caronte and his dwarf assistant. Caronte and the dwarf have killed and removed the brains of three scientists who have the knowledge required to make a neutron bomb. Caronte needs all three brains, since each contains only part of the secret formula necessary to make the bomb. Caronte eventually develops the bomb, but Neutron saves the world from destruction.[16]

By the end of 1963, public discussion about the neutron bomb had subsided. Following the Kennedy administration's decision not to pursue the neutron bomb; the Cuban Missile Crisis in 1962, which made the possibility of nuclear war terrifyingly real; and the signing of the Limited Test Ban Treaty one year later, the issue lay dormant for more than a decade. The breakdown of the broad-based "culture of consensus," which had sustained ever-advancing nuclear weapons development to fight the Cold War, also hastened the disappearance of the neutron death ray from public discourse.[17]

But the issue would not die. The first inklings of a renewed interest in the neutron bomb came in a January 27, 1974, story in the *New York Times*. The article noted that the U.S. government was once again considering developing neutron weapons. Despite this revelation, the public debate did not erupt until June 1977 when an article in the *Washington Post* by journalist Walter Pincus revealed that congressional funding for the neutron bomb had been buried in an appropriations bill. A month later President Jimmy Carter announced his support for neutron bomb development. However, in the face of pressure from North Atlantic Treaty Organization (NATO) allies and the Soviet Union, the latter of which had initiated a large-scale publicity campaign against the "capitalist bomb," Carter reversed his stance a year later.[18] After taking office in 1981, Ronald Reagan yet again reversed Carter's policy, announcing in August that the United States would begin production of neutron warheads.[19]

The resurrection of the neutron bomb in the public mind in the late 1970s coincided with a more general renewal of concern about nuclear issues in U.S. culture. This reawakening had a decidedly antinuclear slant. The shift in mood was sparked by, among other things, the near catastrophe at the Three Mile Island nuclear facility in 1979, the failure of the Salt II Treaty, and a recrudescence of the Cold War in the early years of the Reagan administration.[20] The second time around, American culture confronted the neutron bomb in a much more vigorous manner than it had previously. Although many worried that the N-bomb might lower the threshold of nuclear war, the main concern about the neutron bomb focused on the moral implications of a weapon that killed people and left things untouched.

In the *New York Times Magazine*, columnist Russell Baker referred to the neutron bomb as the "Son of H-Bomb," and an accompanying cartoon featured a little bomb resting in a baby carriage. Baker called the H-bomb's offspring a "nasty little fellow" developed by those who desired a nuclear weapon "which after being exploded would leave the premises neat."[21] Similarly, the leftist newspaper the *Guardian* highlighted the bomb's sanitary killing power. An October 1977 issue featured a cartoon of a family of skeletons, complete with a pet dog, seated around a television set—all victims of a neutron bomb attack.[22]

The alternative news magazine *New Times* also denounced the clean-killing bomb. A 1977 lead story entitled "Learning to Love the Neutron Bomb" featured a cover showing President Carter waving a cowboy hat and straddling a bomb in the manner of Major Kong's apocalyptic bronc ride in *Dr. Strangelove*. The article by Robert Sam Anson began with a chilling description of death by neutron irradiation: "You would not feel it at first, any more than you would feel an X-ray going into your body." You might then begin to feel quite ill, Anson noted, but perhaps would seem to feel healthier once again. However, the symptoms would return shortly in a much more aggressive fashion. Your decline would be rapid and irreversible. Anson continued, "What had killed you was something you couldn't see, a particle of energy smaller than the atom itself. The name for it is neutron." This "creepy" weapon killed people and left buildings unscathed. "That was the beauty of the neutron bomb," Anson declared, "and that was the terror."[23]

Neutron bomb concerns also made their way into television. ABC's science fiction show *Battlestar Galactica* incorporated the neutron bomb into one episode as an explanation for the genocide of the inhabitants of a planet called Paradeen. The episode, entitled "Greetings From Earth," aired on February 25, 1979, and featured the recovery of human beings from a "sleeper ship." The humans are taken to the planet Paradeen, where they discover that the entire population of a once great city has been annihilated by a neutron bomb attack launched by their enemies, the Eastern Alliance. Only two androids survived the attack, and one of them explains that "it's really very simple. The people were destroyed, the buildings weren't. They're as good as new." Viewers also learn that Terra, the humans' home world, was once "a planet of many nations" but that it split into two warring sides—the Eastern Alliance and the Western Alliance—suggesting a parallel to earth's Cold War division between East and West. The black-shirted and jack-booted "commandant" of an Eastern Alliance destroyer further suggests a connection between neutron technology and Nazi genocidal ideology.[24] As we will see, *Battlestar Galactica* was not alone in drawing this analogy.

The neutron bomb also received attention in a made-for-television movie of Captain America, loosely based on the popular Marvel comic book hero. The movie follows the adventures of Steve Rogers, son of the original Captain

The wizard of rock by Lucian K. Truscott IV □ Aborting abortion reform
Freaking out in the control tower □ Kissing off celebrity journalism
A new movie from Disney □ Abby Rockefeller and her toilet by Arthur Lubow

AUGUST 5, 1977 $1.00
THE FEATURE NEWS MAGAZINE

NewTimes

LEARNING
TO LOVE THE
NEUTRON
BOMB
BY ROBERT
SAM ANSON

U.S. ARMY

4.2 Cover of New Times, *August 1977.*

America. Rogers has recently left the Marine Corps and in true 1970s fashion wants nothing more than to sketch beach scenes and "kick back and find out who I am." Unfortunately for Rogers, his plans are dashed when bad guys almost kill him. Fortunately, he is saved from certain death by an injection of a super steroid—called FLAG—developed by his late father and administered by the good folks at the "National Security Lab." FLAG is the very stuff that had given Rogers's father, Captain America the elder, his amazing powers. The lab's director, Simon Mills, attempts to persuade Rogers to follow in his father's super-footsteps, but the reluctant hero is convinced to heed the call only after his close friend (a scientist working on America's neutron bomb program, code-named Project Zeus) is murdered and the scientist's daughter and a sexy lab doctor are kidnapped.

The kidnapper is one Lou Brackett, head of the Andreas Oil Company, who is developing a neutron bomb of his own. After stealing an essential formula from the Zeus project, Brackett and an insolent young scientist develop a neutron bomb. Brackett plans to detonate the bomb in Phoenix, Arizona, so he can abscond with the $1.4 billion in gold held at the Phoenix International Gold Repository. The neutron bomb is essential to his devilish plan because, in the words of Mills, "a neutron bomb only kills people, the gold will be intact." Fortunately for the residents of the Valley of the Sun, Rogers successfully thwarts the neutron attack.

Through its choice of arch-villain, *Captain America* echoes the critique of the neutron bomb as the ultimate capitalist weapon. Brackett is not a foreign terrorist or a diabolical madman but simply an industrialist (i.e., capitalist) who finds in the neutron bomb an ideal way to get rid of the people so he can get his hands on the things he desires. As Mills points out, Brackett is "no mad dog killer." He is, rather, a methodical, capitalist killer.[25]

On the big screen, a handful of American films also tackled the neutron bomb as a subject. *Survival Zone* (1982) is a postapocalypse film set after neutron bombs have devastated the earth. Survivors live in zones like Eden Farm, where the community's leader, a man suggestively named Adam Strong, fights "neo-Nazi marauders."[26] In the 1985 film *Hell Squad,* a crack team of Las Vegas showgirl-commandos is called into action to rescue an American ambassador's son from Middle Eastern terrorists who demand the secret of the "ultra neutron bomb" as ransom.[27] The film opens with actual footage of an atomic blast at the Nevada Test Site. Two researchers in radiation suits, both armed with Geiger counters, survey the scene after the shot. Of all the test animals that were subjected to the blast, nothing remains except for a few horseshoes and the shackles once used to restrain an elephant. One researcher asks, "What are they trying to prove with this new bomb?" to which his companion replies, "that they can destroy humanity but leave the buildings."

The most direct assessment of the "ultra neutron bomb" comes in an exchange between the ambassador and his son after they receive news of the successful test. "I can't believe they actually tested one," says the son, "and not just any one, that god-dammed ultra neutron bomb. . . . [W]hat kind of sick mind could invent a device that kills all life within a certain radius but doesn't even singe a newspaper?" The ambassador, pointing out the window to a scene of women and children digging through ruins, solemnly notes that "if America should engage in a nuclear war, I'd rather we be hit by a bomb that will leave our cities intact for future generations. Why should they have to live like rats trying to rebuild?" For the ambassador, the neutron bomb is ultimately a more humane device than conventional nuclear weapons.

The notion that the neutron bomb was more humane than other nuclear weapons was vigorously rejected by popular music of the period, in particular punk, which offered some of the most pointed critiques of the neutron bomb.[28] In "We Got the Neutron Bomb" (1978), the Los Angeles Punk band the Weirdos linked U.S. development of the neutron bomb to American arrogance and unilateral actions in Europe. The song stated that the "United Nations and NATO won't do / It's just the red, white and blue / We got the neutron bomb," and the song's assertion that "we don't want it, we don't want / Don't blame me" spoke to the sense of impotence and outrage felt by anti–neutron bomb activists. The song also mirrored contemporary critiques of the bomb and the culture that had created it—a culture that seemed to value things more than people.[29]

The neutron bomb particularly appealed to Punk artists because it reflected their nihilism and identification with the apocalyptic, as well as their denunciation of anything deemed "fascist" and their association of "consumer culture with death culture."[30] Another California Punk band, the Dead Kennedys, sarcastically attacked what its members saw as the callous nature of a government that would develop such a weapon. Their 1980 song "Kill the Poor" pointed to an even more sinister potential use of the neutron bomb. Although such a weapon made "no sense in war," it made "perfect sense at home" because it could be used to rid the United States of its homeless and poor.[31]

If the neutron bomb found its way into music, television, and film in the late 1970s, it also served as the subject for a number of novels. Set during the Soviet war against the Afghans, Peter Niesewand's spy-action thriller *Scimitar* follows the efforts of two U.S. Defense Intelligence Agency (DIA) agents to bring back proof (in the form of soil, leaves, and even victims) that the Soviets had detonated a neutron bomb in a remote region of Afghanistan. In the novel, the Afghans erroneously believe they had been subjected to a Soviet chemical weapons attack. The two American agents fall victim to a second neutron bombing, although just how much damage they suffered and how long they would live is left open-ended at the book's conclusion.

General Lyndon Yardley, *Scimitar*'s fictional DIA chief, voices an argument similar to that expressed by Sam Cohen—the neutron bomb's chief advocate—and other actual American analysts who denounced what they saw as an unreasonable fear of the neutron bomb. "As if," Yardley notes, "it's crueler to kill a tank crew with radiation than by giving them third degree burns with a conventional shell so they die screaming two weeks later, or cut them half to pieces with shrapnel. Still that's the great Western public for you."[32] At another point in the novel, one of the DIA agents decries the neutron bomb as an "awful weapon," to which his fellow agent counters: "Is the neutron bomb worse than napalm? Is it worse than those things the Soviets have been using in Afghanistan," which send out "a million sticky things which bond on to people's skin, or clothes, and can't be pulled off? And then they burst into flame?"[33]

Whereas *Scimitar* offers an essentially conservative assessment of the neutron bomb, Kurt Vonnegut's novel *Deadeye Dick* (1982) explores the darker implications of the N-bomb. In the novel the hapless protagonist, Rudy Waltz, gains the sobriquet "Deadeye Dick" after firing a shot from a rifle blindly into the air and accidentally killing a pregnant housewife. The bullet that claims the woman's life appears out of the blue, as it were, taking her life but not stopping the vacuum cleaner she was using at the time. Rudy is subsequently detained by the police, and while he is at the station, officers abuse him physically and verbally. The officers even invite Mr. Metzger, husband of the slain woman, to do what he will with Rudy. But rather than beat, kill, or even blame him, Metzger blames the weapons. Metzger is the editor of the local newspaper, and he later opines on the front page: "My wife has been killed by a machine [a firearm] . . . it makes the blackest of all human wishes come true at once, at a distance: that something die. There is evil for you."[34]

Later, after a grown Rudy has moved to Haiti, a neutron bomb—perhaps accidentally, perhaps not—detonates in his hometown of Midland City, Ohio, leaving the city buildings intact but killing all the people. The city becomes a ghost town. The U.S. government immediately declares that the bombing was not an attack by a foreign power but was caused by a "friendly bomb," one "made in America."[35] The "accidental" neutron bombing of Midland City mobilizes farmers in outlying areas to organize the "Farmers of Southwestern Ohio for Nuclear Sanity." They develop a theory that the bombing was no accident but rather was a deliberate attack by an unnamed and unnameable "clique" within the government or perhaps by the Ku Klux Klan (KKK), which wants to depopulate Midland City so it can use the city to reinstitute slavery in the United States using Haitian refugees as slaves.[36]

In *Deadeye Dick* Vonnegut cleverly links Rudy's indiscriminate shot across the city with the neutron bomb. Both the accidental bombing and the accidental shooting are senseless and lethal to human life. Vonnegut also probes the potential fascist and racist implications of the neutron bomb. When Rudy is detained by the police, one officer refers to him as "Mr. Rich Nazi Shitface" because Rudy's father had once been a friend and supporter of Adolf Hitler. The connection is further strengthened by the uncovering of a possible KKK-government conspiracy to reestablish slavery in the United States.[37]

The linking of neutron bomb technology with race and domestic intervention had been made earlier by strategic analyst Daniel Ellsberg when he spoke to an anti–neutron bomb rally in Amsterdam. Best known for leaking the Pentagon Papers to the *New York Times* in 1971, Ellsberg noted that the real beneficiaries of the neutron bomb were those who owned or controlled the property in the targeted area and "whose enemies are the people of the area, that is, their own countrymen." Thus, Ellsberg maintained, the neutron bomb was "basically a counterinsurgency weapon. . . . [L]ater models of the bomb with reduced blast and reduced fission products will be appropriate for such purposes not only in Johannesburg but even within Western Europe."[38] The N-bomb might be used not only to "kill the poor" but also to eliminate internal political enemies and racial and ethnic minorities.

When in *Deadeye Dick* Rudy observes that 100,000 people were killed but all the televisions at the Holiday Inn near ground zero were still working, he wonders if "it matters to anyone or anything that all those peepholes [Vonnegut's metaphor for lives] were closed so suddenly? Since all the property is undamaged, has the world lost anything it loved?"[39] Here Vonnegut is articulating a major critique of the bomb that kills people but saves property as well as criticizing the American culture of things that created the monstrous weapon in the first place.[40]

Patrick Meyers's play *K2* presents a similar vision of the neutron bomb. First staged in New York in March 1983, the play centers on two mountain climbers stranded on K2, the world's second-highest peak. One of the men has broken his leg; and following an avalanche and the loss of much of their equipment, the two face an uncertain fate. Thus stranded, the men ponder such questions as the nature of God, physics, and personal relationships. Harold, a physicist at Lawrence Radiation Lab, relates to his fellow mountaineer, Taylor, his "gizmo theory," which posits a world governed by "Gizmo Kings" and "Doodad Barons." "If you were given the choice of developing a bomb that would blow away all the things . . . or of developing a bomb that blew away all of the people and left all of the things, which would you choose?" Harold asks.

Taylor correctly surmises that he is talking about the neutron bomb. Harold, who had worked on developing the bomb at Lawrence, explains that the neutron bomb is "the Great Gadget, the protector and sustainer of all gadgets . . . the one that is designed to decimate all life without so much as scratching any of the precious little gizmos crammed on our earth." It is, he points out, "the culmination of Gizmo Madness."[41]

Harold's query to Taylor in *K2* considers the neutron bomb in terms of a tragic irony, one other observers had also noted. If scientists could construct a bomb that kills people but leaves things untouched, why could they not make one that destroys things but does not harm people? A 1977 cartoon in the *Los Angeles Times* pondered the possibility of a more discriminate neutron bomb, an "improved neutron bomb," that would kill soldiers and leave civilians alone or perhaps even kill only politicians and leave everyone else unharmed.[42] More recently, Gore Vidal's novel *The Smithsonian Institution* (1998) raised a similar question. When the novel's young math genius—nicknamed "T."—works out formulas for an atomic bomb, a neutron bomb, and a "*non*lethal bomb," his latter idea is quickly dismissed. As one character asks, "[W]hat's the point to a bomb that doesn't kill the enemy?"[43]

The "point" of the neutron bomb is probed more deeply in David Rabe's play *Hurlyburly* (1984). Rabe's character Eddie dubs the neutron bomb the "Thing that loves things," a reflection of a society that values possessions more than people. Eddie notes that the neutron bomb "has got ATTITUDE" and that "inherent in the conception of it is this fucking ATTITUDE about what is worthwhile in the world and what is worth preserving." Echoing the gizmo society theory presented by Harold in *K2,* Eddie points out that the "fastidious prick" that sits at the top of this order is "THINGS!" One bomb would kill everyone in his apartment, but, Eddie notes, all of his furnishings would remained untouched: "The chairs, the table . . . the Things are un-fucking disturbed. It annihilates people and saves THINGS. It loves things. It is a thing that loves things."[44]

Rabe's play drives to the heart of why so many Americans responded so vigorously against the neutron bomb in the years 1977–1983. Americans confronted the bomb that loves things and annihilates people. To be sure, the neutron bomb provoked controversy because it was yet another nuclear weapon and seemed to make nuclear war more likely. But concern over the neutron bomb ran deeper than that. Critics of the bomb saw it as the offspring of a callous society that cared more for property than for people. Some even suggested that the "thing" might be used at home against fellow Americans.

In some ways, the manner in which American culture reacted to the neutron bomb in the late 1970s and early 1980s had been anticipated two decades earlier when it first reached the public's attention. At that time Americans worried about the implications of the death-ray device and expressed those concerns through such avenues as popular magazines. Yet they did not reach the same conclusions that were reached during the second phase of the controversy. The N-bomb was not seen as symptomatic of a crass, materialistic society, and the implication that it was best suited for domestic purposes or racial genocide would have seemed absurd. Americans of the late 1950s and early 1960s understood the weapon as a fantastic new death ray, another startling breakthrough in nuclear technology.

Things had changed by 1977 when the neutron bomb resurfaced. The hope for a bright atomic future, of futuristic death rays and atomic-powered spaceships, and the belief in the fundamental rightness of the American way had been eclipsed by fears of clean-killing bombs and criticisms of the capitalist society from which they sprang. High Atomic Culture had given way to Late Atomic Culture. The breakdown of Cold War consensus, a growing antinuclear movement, and an increasing awareness of the legacy of nuclear testing and the arms race had changed the cultural context. Long gone was the hope of America leading the way into a shining atomic future—the neutron bomb helped explode all that.

NOTES

I thank Ferenc Szasz and Alexander Prusin for their helpful comments and suggestions. Thanks also to the students in my spring 2002 Atomic America class for their insightful critiques of an earlier draft of this chapter.

1. William Laurence, "The Neutron Bomb," *Saturday Evening Post,* May 5, 1962, 52.

2. *Forbidden Planet,* dir. Fred Wilcox, MGM, 1956.

3. Margot Henriksen has argued that *Dr. Strangelove's* "focus on the nuclear establishment and its fomenting of Armageddon symbolize the culture of dissent's shift to open criticism of the past and present consensual atomic system. The apocalyptic ending of *Dr. Strangelove* as well as the film's refusal to abandon its dark laughter even in the face of apocalypse denote the end of the fear and intimidation previously exercised by the culture of consensus." Henriksen further notes that "between 1963 and 1964 the apocalyptic imagination of the culture of dissent merged with the apocalyptic reality of a society confronted by events like the missile crisis and Kennedy's assassination, and the American system itself faced internal apocalypse and dissolution." Margot Henriksen, *Dr. Strangelove's America: Society and Culture in the Atomic Age* (Berkeley: University of California Press, 1997), xxv, 305.

4. *Time,* June 3, 1957, 65.

5. *Time,* November 30, 1959, 15.

6. *U.S. News and World Report,* May 30, 1960, 56.

7. *Time,* February 10, 1961, 16.

8. *Newsweek,* April 4, 1960, 66.

9. Freeman Dyson, "The Future Development of Nuclear Weapons," *Foreign Affairs* 38 (April 1960): 458–460.

10. Martin Mann, "Death-Ray Bomb," *Popular Science* (August 1960): 15–16.

11. Martin Mann, "U.S. Crash-Programs Decisive Nuclear Weapon: The Death Ray Bomb," *Popular Science* (January 1962): 90–91, 208–209.

12. James Biery, "Keeping Up With the Atom," *Popular Mechanics* (August 1960): 28.

13. Laurence, "The Neutron Bomb," 53–55.

14. Ibid., 53, 56.

15. *The Poisoned Earth,* dir. Casper Wrede, 1961; Mick Broderick, *Nuclear Movies* (Jefferson, NC: McFarland, 1988), 98.

16. Broderick, *Nuclear Movies,* 96.

17. On the breakdown of the culture of consensus, see Henriksen, *Dr. Strangelove's America,* xxv.

18. Soviet writer Evgeni Dolmatovsky's "Dirty Tricks With a 'Clean' Bomb" was typical of the Soviet public stance on an American neutron bomb: "It is not any accident that they have borrowed the term [property] used by businessmen and property-owners to describe a weapon of mass destruction. The advocates and owners of the neutron bomb are simply true to themselves. It is easy to kill millions of people by radiation, a human being isn't worth much after all, is he?! The factories, bridges and perhaps even the shacks will not crumble down, while mansions and palaces are sure to survive. Property, indeed!" Evgeni Dolmatovsky, "Dirty Tricks With a 'Clean' Bomb," *Soviet Literature* 12 (December 1977): 157.

19. Sam Cohen, *The Truth About the Neutron Bomb: The Inventor of the Bomb Speaks Out* (New York: William Morrow, 1983), 118.

20. On the cultural reawakening of nuclear concern, especially as it pertains to film, see Toni Perrine, *Film and the Nuclear Age: Representing Cultural Anxiety* (New York: Garland, 1998), 12–13.

21. Russell Baker, "Son of H-Bomb," *New York Times Magazine,* July 31, 1977, 6.

22. The *Guardian,* October 12, 1977.

23. Robert Sam Anson, "Learning to Love the Neutron Bomb," *New Times,* August 5, 1977, 24–25.

24. *Battlestar Galactica,* "Greetings From Earth," ABC, February 25, 1979.

25. *Captain America,* dir. Rod Holcomb, Universal City Studios, 1979.

26. Broderick, *Nuclear Movies,* 154.

27. *Hell Squad,* dir. Kenneth Hartford, Cinevid, 1985.

28. In my analysis of Punk music I agree with Jude Davies who takes " 'a common sense' literary reading of lyrics," with "particular attention to the subject positions as a self-conscious attempt to cope with the problematization of politics and transcendence brought about by commodity culture and mid-70s disillusionment

with the post-war 'consensus.'" Jude Davies, "The Future of 'No Future': Punk Rock and Postmodern Theory," *Journal of Popular Culture* 29, 4 (1996): 4.

29. Weirdos, "We Got the Neutron Bomb," Dangerhouse, 1978.

30. Davies, "The Future of 'No Future,'" 13. Roger Sabin draws a distinction between what he calls Punk's identification with "negationism" and nihilism; Roger Sabin, ed., *Punk Rock: So What? The Cultural Legacy of Punk* (London: Routledge, 1999), 3. A fine example of the connection between nuclear weapons and fascism is found in the Sex Pistols' "God Save the Queen": "God save the Queen / The fascist regime / Made you a moron / potential H-bomb," *Never Mind the Bullocks Here's the Sex Pistols,* Virgin, 1977.

31. Dead Kennedys, "Kill the Poor," Cherry Red, 1980.

32. Peter Niesewand, *Scimitar* (Briarcliff Manor, NY: Stein and Day, 1984), 7.

33. Ibid., 44.

34. Kurt Vonnegut Jr., *Deadeye Dick* (New York: Dell, 1982), 87.

35. Ibid., 226, 229.

36. Ibid., 150, 232–234.

37. Ibid., 85, 240.

38. Ellsberg's speech is reported in the *Nation,* May 27, 1978, 633.

39. Vonnegut, *Deadeye Dick,* 34.

40. In her review of *Deadeye Dick,* Loree Rackstraw points out that Vonnegut's work offers the possibility "for us to cut through the glaze of false hope that blinds us to the truth of our own self-destructive history." Loree Rackstraw, "The Vonnegut Cosmos," in Robert Merrill, ed., *Critical Essays on Kurt Vonnegut* (Boston: G. K. Hall, 1990), 54.

41. Patrick Meyers, *K2* (Garden City, NY: Nelson Doubleday, 1982), 23–24.

42. The cartoon is reprinted in Cohen, *The Truth About the Neutron Bomb,* 114.

43. Gore Vidal, *The Smithsonian Institution* (New York: Random House, 1998), 45.

44. David Rabe, *Hurlyburly and Those the River Keeps: Two Plays by David Rabe* (New York: Grove, 1995 [1984]), 305–306.

The Nuclear Past in the Landscape Present

PETER GOIN

Most people passing through Nevada on its highways perceive this landscape as an enormous expanse of arid, brown, and empty desert—in short, visually tedious. I must be an anomaly, however. Nearly twenty years ago, I became fascinated with basin and range country. Most of Nevada is under the jurisdiction of the U.S. government and is therefore open for camping, exploring, hunting, photographing, and numerous other outdoor activities. Except for the Nevada Test Site. This 1,350-square-mile government testing area is the largest fenced, "off-limits" section in the state. Two decades of nuclear tests, both above-ground and belowground, replete with mushroom clouds and subsidence craters define the site and perhaps the state.

During the 1980s I had been told it was impossible to gain access to photograph the Nevada Test Site. Nuclear explosions, albeit underground, were still happening. In those days protestors avoiding armed military guards were trespassing onto ground zeroes, disrupting planned detonations. Announcements of nuclear tests were delayed because of these tactics, and a veil of secrecy was draped over the test site. The simple question "what does this landscape really look like" remained. Finally, after a long and difficult negotiation, the Department of Energy granted me permission to photograph within the Nevada Test Site.

As I crossed through the gates at Mercury, gateway to the test site, the landscape—recognizable because of the familiarity of historical and publicity films—provoked a feeling unlike the usual Nevada basin and range. Perhaps this feeling was created by a sense of prior exclusion and mystery. The landscape was charged, literally and figuratively, and that irony was present in my mind. On that particular day the winds were calm, but the temperature exceeded 100 degrees Fahrenheit. This kind of landscape—profound in what it represents, politically controversial, secluded from visual access—provokes a similar response to the one I experience when I cross an international boundary. In such cases I become self-conscious, primarily aware of the foreign quality and nature of the landscape. At the test site the physical threat, ubiquitous yet vague, informed my response. Radioactivity is not a visible phenomenon and is obviously pervasive at the site. I cannot see, hear, smell, or feel it. A few accounts suggest that during excessive contamination a person may experience a slight metallic taste. I swallowed, tasting dryness more than anything else. A roadway is fenced on both sides, clearly posted with *danger—radioactive area* signs. Is the roadway, surrounded by radioactivity, safe from contamination? Subsidence craters are everywhere. Is a slight depression a contaminated subsidence crater, or is it a simple earthen depression that I am interpreting as dangerous?

Frenchman Flat is littered with the remains of earlier aboveground tests. These structures, ruins, relics, and indestructible refuse have become environmental ART in an unintentional way, primarily because of their significance as metaphorical and visual artifacts of the nuclear era. I keep thinking that these objects—from tanks to doom town houses to aluminum domes—will reveal truths about the nature of the atom, of history, about ourselves, but they maintain a silence to an almost unimaginable force detonated years ago. My guide decides not to leave the vehicle and nervously watches his clock. I am told I have no more than two minutes, and I attempt a world speed record on 4×5 photography. The winds may have been calm, but my heart raced. The dust that collected on my boots made me nervous. The hot, bright light made me squint, even with dark glasses. The risks were obvious but somehow necessary. The yellow (generic for contamination) ropes and posts were everywhere. Burial signs, "gardens," and radioactive notices are commonplace—so much so that I started to consider their placement normal, or at least expected. I was glad when I was back on highway 95 heading toward Reno. I remembered Tom Lehrer's lyrics about the cowboy riding around the test site in his lead BVDs but could not remember the melody.

Each of the nuclear sites—the Nevada Test Site, the Trinity Site, and Hanford—provokes a similar response. Although each site is unique, they share the common thread of restricted access and radioactive risk. Although no longer producing fissionable products, the Hanford Nuclear Reservation suffers from severe radioactive contamination. The nature and scale of ground contamination is beyond easy imagination. The Trinity Site contains radioactive Trinitite. Nuclear landscapes are landscapes of fear.

"The Nuclear Past in the Landscape Present" provides ten comparative photographic pairs for visual analysis and reflection. Normally derived from a preexisting (historical) photograph, precise rephotography requires that the photographer use the exact tripod position, camera format, lens and film type, and angle of view, as well as the same time of day, year, and weather conditions. However, the comparative views in this chapter were created differently, not linearly from the historical photograph to the rephotograph but from the contemporary view looking back into archives. Clearly, this necessitates a flexible interpretation of the conventional rules governing precise rephotography and explains why the views are similar at best and not in any case exact.

The comparison between two photographs, made of the same subject or even of a similar subject, magnifies the passage and distortion(s) of time. Each photograph isolates a brief fragment, less than a second, almost like a dot on a map; two dots determine a connecting line. In this case the line divides time and not geography, reflecting the effects and influences of profound human interaction. This rephotography project places both the contemporary and the historical photographs in a new context, changing the importance and meaning of the subject within the photograph. The original photographer's intent in making the photograph is subordinated to, or appropriated within, a different matrix, encouraging our focus on the understanding and study of (historical) landscape change. This project offers simulacra in two distinct yet similar photographs, transcending the particular criteria of each exposure. The meaning of each photograph is dependent upon the other.

The photographs are basically artifacts. But because each photograph (historical versus contemporary) represents a different conceptual premise, this project is dependent upon the available historical materials while at the same time transcending their original purpose. The photographs function on many levels—as documents, but they also elevate the objects within the photographs to iconographic significance.

Events occurring between two fixed moments separated by fifty or sixty years may erode the fear and the memories these landscapes embody. The photographs capture only brief periods of time, but the objects—and I hope the photographs—have evolved into a visual legacy that demonstrates the irony and subliminal effect of fear these nuclear landscapes provoke. Barring this, these photographs should at least provide visual evidence of these evolving nuclear lands, and readers can make their own decision about "what the landscape looks like."[1] The nuclear past is within the landscape present.

NOTES

1. This chapter is derived in part from the body of the text of my book *Nuclear Landscapes* (Baltimore: Johns Hopkins University Press, 1991). Some of these photographs are included in the book, but many have never been published until now.

5.1 Aerial view of Trinity Site twenty-eight hours after detonation. Courtesy, *United States Department of Energy.*

5.2 Trinity Site, the site of the world's first nuclear explosion on July 16, 1945 at 5:29:45 A.M. Mountain War Time near White Sands, New Mexico, on the Alamorgordo Bombing Range in the Jornada del Muerto Desert, where the dawn of the nuclear age began.

On a hot, windy summer day in July 1988, I crossed the boundary into a U.S. military installation, into a landscape previously avoided and fenced with "no trespassing" signs. This simple act of legal trespass created its own environment of anticipation. The words ground zero *signify a dangerous, fearful, even catastrophic place. My U.S. Air Force guide, a colonel, was ready and waiting and asked me if I realized that Trinity Site had been bulldozed and fenced but that little else remained—except an obelisk marker. He was right, but only on the surface. Consider the anomaly of the usual desert scrub, a slight earthly depression, perhaps 400 yards in diameter, surrounded by a tall chain-link fence. Except for the obelisk, the landscape revealed few visual clues that indicated the flurry of top-secret activity so many years ago. Here rests, however, the most important site of contemporary sublime—that combination of awe and terror memorialized in nineteenth-century art representing the conquest of the western United States. Here is the center of the nuclear era, I remember thinking to myself. As I wandered about the outer perimeter my guide picked up some greenish rock, flat, glasslike, and offered these fragments to me as a souvenir. "Take them," he said. "These are some of the rarest rocks on earth—Trinitite, created when that first atomic explosion fused the desert sand into green glass." I accepted his offer and remember thinking about "touching history" as I put the glassy rock into my breast pocket. Yes, the rocks are still radioactive.*

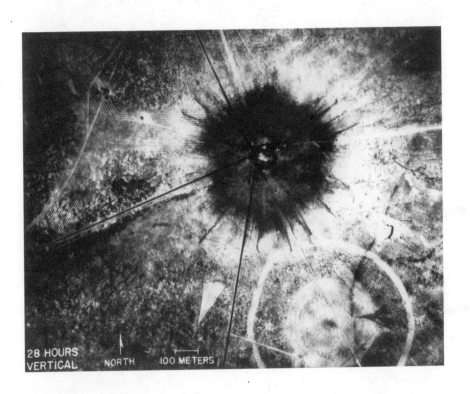

28 HOURS
VERTICAL NORTH 100 METERS

5.3 Weather-worn and deserted, the George McDonald ranch house served inconspicuously as a highly dangerous nuclear site—the rancher's home where the world's first nuclear bomb was assembled. Only two miles from ground zero, the ranch house survived the Trinity Site detonation with minimal damage. In the ensuing years, the uninhabited house, which lies within the boundaries of White Sands Missile Range, fell into disrepair. Walking through the rooms provoked thoughts about the scientists' ghosts working secretly, under deadline, suffering from potentially serious radiation exposure. Hymer Friedell, from the Manhattan District's medical office, summed up the situation by saying "The idea was to explode the damned thing. . . . We weren't terribly concerned with the radiation" (quoted in Barton C. Hacker, The Dragon's Tail, *Berkeley: University of California Press, 1987, pp. 84–85). My guide showed me the plans for the renovation of the ranch house—homage to its historical importance. Photograph circa 1963–1964, courtesy U.S. Army, White Sands Missile Range, photographer unknown.*

5.4 In 1982, the U.S. Army stabilized the house to prevent further damage. Under the auspices of the Department of Energy and the U.S. Army, the National Park Service completely restored the house so that it would appear as it did on July 12, 1945. George McDonald Ranch House, Trinity Site National Historic Landmark. Photograph circa 1984, courtesy U.S. Army, White Sands Missile Range, photographer unknown.

5.5 White Bluffs, Washington, view east toward Columbia River, circa 1940. Commercial Hotel is the building on left. During the late 1930s Hanford and White Bluffs were small but successful agricultural communities nestled in a bend of the Columbia River about twenty-five miles from the Oregon border in eastern Washington. White Bluffs, named after the 300-foot-high bluffs lining the Columbia River, had a population of about 200. The residents considered themselves dedicated, hardworking pioneers. Courtesy, United States Department of Energy, Hanford Site.

5.6 Main Street, White Bluffs Town Site, June 1988. White Bluffs and Hanford were chosen as the site for the world's first nuclear reactor because the population was relatively small and isolated, the Columbia River provided the many thousands of gallons of water per minute needed to cool the reactors, railroads were already in place, and the Grand Coulee Dam supplied the electrical power. The federal government "condemned" the land and began to relocate the 1,200 people who lived in the two towns and surrounding area. Because of the government's authority, landowners had little recourse but to accept its offer. By September 26, 1944, just eighteen months after construction began, the world's first nuclear reactor—called the "B Reactor"—began producing plutonium. By the following summer, enough plutonium had been produced to manufacture two nuclear weapons. Hanford plutonium was used in the Trinity detonation and for the bomb that exploded over Nagasaki on August 9, 1945. The legacy of radioactive contamination contextualizes these communities as ruins of the nuclear era. This abandoned street in a condemned town is inhabited now only by coyotes, ground squirrels, and skunks . . . ah yes, the skunks. I thought the subliminal fear of radioactive contamination would be oppressive, but a passing skunk claimed territory as I was making this image. I asked my guide if he knew how much leached radioactivity wound up in the plants and animals, especially in the skunks. Pausing as if to imagine, he did not answer, and soon we drove on to the next site.

5.7 Built in 1907 and operated by W. J. Kincaid, the White Bluffs Bank featured a modern vault. The bank closed in the early 1940s. Courtesy, United States Department of Energy, Hanford Site.

5.8 First Bank of White Bluffs, June 1998. The bank operated from 1909 to 1943.

5.9 Hanford's High School building was built in 1916 but burned on December 28, 1936. It reopened in fall of 1938 with a new gymnasium on the left. The renovation would be short-lived, as Hanford was condemned only a few years later, in 1943. Courtesy, United States Department *of Energy, Hanford Site.*

5.10 Hanford High School (1916–1943), June 1998.

5.11 Nevada Test Site. "NATO observers observing BOLTZMANN (May 28, 1957). The Boltzmann shot was weapons related, detonated from a tower at a yield of 12 kilotons. Courtesy, *United States Department of Energy National Nuclear Security Administration.*

5.12 Nevada Test Site, July 1996. Bleachers with approximately a nine-mile view of Frenchman Flat, used for witnessing aboveground atomic explosions. The bleachers are located on the east side of Mercury Highway. Most visitors to the Nevada Test Site are unaware that these benches are still here, as they cannot be seen from the highway.

5.13 Nevada Test Site. "*Dome type structures, larger than the one shown in the foreground above, have been proposed as an effective and economic means of providing mass shelter. Under Federal Civil Defense Administration auspices, three dome shelters, 50 feet in diameter, will undergo nuclear blast at approximate overpressure ranges of from 20 to 70 pounds per square inch (psi). The reinforced concrete domes, of 6-inch constant shell thickness, will be exposed to blast without the aid of earth cover. FCDA engineers decided the 50 feet diameter structure (above) was adequate for prelimi-nary tests, eliminating the expense of a 150-ft. structure. A temporary steel door will close off the structure. A full-size, prototype steel shelter door, designed to close off a dome shelter of about 150 ft. in diameter, will be tested independently. The trenches on the right have no relationship to the shelter, being cable trenches*"; explanatory text that accompanies the historic photograph. Courtesy, United States Department of Energy National Nuclear Security Administration.

5.14 Nevada Test Site, Frenchman Flat, area of aboveground testing debris, July 1996. When I photographed in this area, I was told the alpha particles, if inhaled, would be harmful. The health and safety supervisor restricted—to only two minutes—the time I could be on the flat playa. My guide stayed in the vehicle with the windows rolled all the way up. Using a 4×5 field view camera, I had to work fast. I often joke that I must hold the world's land-speed record for 4×5 photography. My boots were covered with the alkali, and I held my breath when the winds blew.

5.15 One of the houses used in the atomic test code-named "Annie." This house, although not the same house shown below as part of the "Apple II" test, does show the pretest appearance of this type of construction. Caption UK-53-01, courtesy, United States Department of Energy National Nuclear Security Administration.

5.16 Doom town. This building was part of a "doom town," consisting of houses, office buildings, fallout shelters, power systems, communications equipment, a radio broadcasting station, and trailer homes. This house was 7,500 feet from ground zero. In a test called "Apple II," fired on May 5, 1955, the entire foundation shifted from the force of the 29-kiloton blast. The house has been partially restored to document the historical importance of the aboveground testing period. Coincidentally, the house is subject to continued Historic Preservation funds, creating an ironic context for the destructiveness of nuclear weapons. Ubiquitous film sequences of similar houses exploding reinforce the significance of this remaining house.

5.17 Sedan test was fired on July 6, 1962. "Heavier particles began falling back to earth as the main cloud continued to rise. The base surge of dust began to roll along the desert floor"; explanatory text that accompanies the historic photograph. Courtesy, United States Department of Energy National Nuclear Security Administration.

5.18 Sedan Crater remains from the Plowshares program, the purpose of which was to test the peaceful use of nuclear explosions. The operating hypothesis was that a nuclear explosion could easily excavate a large area, facilitating the building of canals and roads, improving mining techniques, or simply moving a large amount of rock and soil. The intensity and distribution of radiation proved too great, and the program was abandoned. The Sedan device was thermonuclear—70 percent fusion, 30 percent fission—with a yield of 100 kilotons. The crater is an impressive 635 feet deep and 1,280 feet wide. The weight of the material lifted was 12 million tons. This crater is one of the highlights of the tour of the Nevada Test Site, serving as a symbol of the transformation from the mundane to the lyrical, from the scientific warrior to the accidental tourist. As I stood on the platform overlooking this impressive crater and tried to find a way to represent it within the confines of a 4×5 negative, my guide assured me that the radioactivity here would be no more than that of a chest X-ray or two. He was not sure.

5.19 Teapot/ESS. The 23 March 1955 subsurface atomic test was the seventh in the Teapot series at Nevada Test Site. This was a weapons-related test, relatively small by comparison, with a yield range of 1 kiloton. Courtesy, United States Department of Energy National Nuclear Security Administration.

5.20 Nevada Test Site, ESS Crater, part of Upshot-Knothole series of aboveground nuclear detonations. View is looking south, July 1996. Craters such as these litter the Nevada Test Site. The dust remains radioactive.

CHAPTER SIX

The Mushroom Cloud as Kitsch

A. COSTANDINA TITUS

Although the term *kitsch* has gained wide currency since the 1930s, both in the United States and abroad, the concept remains problematic. Some see kitsch strictly in relation to the arts, whereas others view it as a historico-sociological phenomenon of the modern age. *Webster's Collegiate Dictionary* defines it simply as "something that appeals to popular or lowbrow tastes and is often of poor quality." Other definitions include kitsch as "the principle of evil in the value of art," the "parody of catharsis," "a specifically aesthetic form of lying," "a time capsule with a two way ticket to the realm of myth," and the "absolute denial of shit," to mention a few.[1] Indeed, attempting to discern the meaning of kitsch is akin to the U.S. Supreme Court's struggle with pornography; as Justice Potter Stewart commented, "I can't define it, but I know it when I see it."[2]

Regardless of how it is delineated by scholars and critics, most people would agree that kitsch is easy to recognize. It is virtually omnipresent throughout the modern world. There is kitsch on sale wherever tourists gather, from Lourdes to the Great Wall. Look up kitsch on the Internet, and on Yahoo alone you will find over 42,000 entries, ranging from Christmas kitsch to kitsch bitch.

This incredible proliferation of kitsch can be attributed to a burgeoning market of people with disposable incomes to spend on nonessentials and to the

101

6.1 "Through Protective Goggles on the U.S.S. Appalachian." Painting of Bikini Blast, www.history.navy.mil/ac/bikini.

development of techniques, first, of mass production and, later, of mass communication. Furthermore, because it is so easily manufactured and so widely distributed, kitsch can be exploited for political as well as commercial purposes and thus can be employed by any regime to generate support for a particular ideology or policy agenda.

An excellent example of American kitsch is the mushroom cloud, which since the bombing of Hiroshima has appeared on familiar objects as diverse as record jackets and coffee mugs, T-shirts and neon signs. Bursting onto the scene in 1945, the mushroom cloud was almost immediately recognized the world over as a symbol of U.S. power. And at home the government quickly promoted it to instill awe and fear in the citizenry and thereby build support for Cold War defense policies. Recently, after virtually disappearing during the détente years when testing moved underground, the mushroom cloud has reemerged and today, ironically, is viewed somewhat wistfully as a nostalgic icon reminiscent of simpler, safer times.

Although much has been written over the last decade analyzing the impact of the atomic bomb on American thought and culture during the 1940s and 1950s, little attention has been paid to the symbolic value of the mushroom cloud itself. This chapter addresses that omission by tracing the evolution of the mushroom cloud from its origins as an instrument of political kitsch to its current reincarnation as a bit of Cold War nostalgic kitsch.

KITSCH AND ART

The term *kitsch,* like the concept it designates, is closely associated with modernity. It came into vogue in the mid-1800s in the jargon of art dealers in Munich and was used to refer to cheap, artistic renderings of street scenes often sold as souvenirs to tourists. As is frequently the case with such loosely constructed and widely circulated labels, its etymology is uncertain. Some believe it derives from the English word *sketch,* mispronounced by Germans, whereas others suggest its possible origin is the German verb *verkitschen,* which means to make cheap, or perhaps the verb *kitschen,* which means to collect rubbish from the street. Expressions in other languages refer to similar concepts, such as *cursi* in Spanish, *schlock* and *schmaltz* in Yiddish, *camelot* and *style pompier* in French, and *poshlost* in Russian; but kitsch has been the only such term to enter the international lexicon.[3]

Most of the early writing on kitsch focuses on the art world. Herman Broch, in a classic essay published in the 1930s, attributed the rise of kitsch to changes in the conception of the aesthetic ideal wrought by romanticism.[4] Likewise, in his influential 1939 piece on kitsch and the avant-garde, noted art critic Clement Greenberg wrote, "[T]he alternative to abstraction is not Michelangelo but kitsch."[5] And by the 1950s Harold Rosenberg felt compelled to proclaim, "[K]itsch has captured all the arts."[6] Twenty years later Hilton Kramer, in a 1974 *New York Times* review of a contemporary American exhibit at the Art Institute of Chicago, lamented the proliferation of kitsch in the works of Andy Warhol and his followers, whom Kramer dubbed "the Flea Market School."[7]

Views of kitsch in postmodern art are less consistently negative. On the one hand, Roger Scruton commented in a 1999 *Urbanites* article that kitsch art is "pretense"; it "converts the higher emotions into a pre-digested and trouble-free form and like processed food passes from junk to crap without an intervening spell of nourishment."[8] Conversely, art critic Robert Nelson, in a 2000 review of William Eicholtz's sculpture, praised kitsch as "a resource, a pool of associations upon which artists can draw in order to enrich the form and content of their images."[9]

POLITICAL KITSCH

Social and psychological studies of kitsch can also be found, albeit less extensively, in the literature on modern culture. T. W. Adorno of the Frankfurt School wrote in the 1940s that kitsch provides the masses with a means of pleasurable escape from the drabness of modern life.[10] In the 1960s such scholars as Dwight MacDonald and Leo Lowenthal began to examine the origins and ethics of mass culture, including the implications of kitsch.[11] Matei Calinescu explored kitsch as an inextricable aspect of modern life in his 1977 book, *Faces of Modernity*.[12] Others interested in cultural relativism during this period include Jenny Sharp, who explained kitsch as a purely middle-class phenomenon, and Susan Sontag, who wrote the definitive essay on "camp"—which is the self-conscious use of kitsch—describing it much like Adorno as "the answer to the problem: how to be a dandy in the age of mass culture."[13]

Interest in the uses and implications of kitsch gained momentum in the 1980s and moved into the political arena with the publication of two very different books, one fiction and one academic. Milan Kundera's novel *The Unbearable Lightness of Being* explores communist kitsch as epitomized by the May Day ceremony and parade and concludes that "in the realm of kitsch, the dictatorship of the heart reigns supreme."[14] Similarly, Saul Friedlander examines fascist symbolism in *Reflections of Nazism: An Essay on Kitsch and Death*.[15] Both works analyze the successful employment of mass-produced images to destroy individualism and promote a particular ideology.

Of special interest is the distinction Friedlander draws between "common" kitsch and "uplifting" kitsch. The common variety is aimed at universality and uniformity, whereas the uplifting version is rooted, symbol-cultured, and emotionally linked to the values of a specific group. Common kitsch serves to promote something—mainly on commercial terms—without cultural restrictions, such as Mickey Mouse. Uplifting kitsch, however, reinforces identification within a specific and well-defined context mainly in ideological terms, such as a May Day parade or a swastika.[16]

According to Friedlander, uplifting kitsch can be easily exploited for political purposes because its inherent qualities lend themselves so readily to effective mobilization of the masses. The message it conveys is simple, straightforward, and thus easily understood by the public. Second, it stimulates an unreflexive and emotional rather than a rational response. Third, it can be mass produced quickly and cheaply and can be both widely marketed and distributed, making it readily accessible to the vast majority of the population. Fourth, it combines aesthetics and politics, using elements of beauty to enhance the values of the regime. And finally, it leads to the stylization of an image, which tends to capture obvious mythical patterns, resulting in a reinforcing congruence between construct and form that pervades the popular culture of a system.

Uplifting or political kitsch often emerges when tradition is destroyed. It helps people cope with traumatic change and endows them with hope by promoting the belief that they can create a better world de novo if they only have the power, the knowledge, and the right-mindedness. Accordingly, it becomes a reinforcing symbol, a bonding force that aestheticizes destruction and makes it acceptable. It reassures the observer, simultaneously providing psychological comfort and reinforcing a host of national mythologies. In short, by tranquilizing the masses, kitsch can facilitate legitimation of the new regime.[17]

Borrowing heavily from Friedlander and Murray Edelman's work on politics and art,[18] Catherine Lugg further explores political kitsch and its relationship to modern U.S. public policy. According to Lugg, kitsch, "as a condensation symbol rooted in bad art, combines elements of history, cultural mythology, and syrupy emotionalism to shape the direction of the political environment and possible policy prescriptions."[19]

In the United States, appreciation for kitsch is cultivated early in public school, which is free, compulsory, and unfortunately can be mind-numbing; it is then reinforced over the years by a host of psychological, political, and cultural vehicles—sometimes known as socializing agents—the most pervasive of which is television. The public is constantly bombarded with symbolic references via advertising, programming, and news broadcasts that reinforce the prevailing ideology.[20] Think of baseball, apple pie, and Chevrolet; Camelot and the War on Poverty; Willie Horton and "Uncle Sam Wants You."

THE MUSHROOM CLOUD AS POLITICAL KITSCH

The U.S. government's persistently glorified depiction of the mushroom cloud throughout the late 1940s and 1950s is an excellent example of the successful exploitation of political kitsch. Symbolizing the awesome power of American scientific and military know-how, the mushroom cloud was promoted by various administrations to generate support for an arms race designed to win the Cold War and save the free world. All the essential elements of Friedlander's uplifting kitsch were present: simple message, mass distribution, emotional response, beautiful imagery, and stylized form.

From the beginning, virtually everyone—young and old alike—recognized the mushroom cloud and knew what it represented. As *Scientific Monthly* reported in September 1945, "Just as people recall the circumstances under which they first heard the news of the attack on Pearl Harbor, so will they remember how the atomic bomb first burst upon their consciousness."[21]

After the bomb was dropped on Hiroshima, the first pictures that appeared on front pages of newspapers and magazines across the country were tightly controlled, official government releases of the mushroom cloud, not of the destruction on the ground in Japan or of the bomb itself. *Life* magazine, with a circulation of over 5 million, devoted much of its August 20, 1945, issue to the bomb with full-page photographs of the towering mushroom-shaped cloud.

Clearly, the message was not only simple and direct but widely disseminated and easily understood.

The public's reaction to the scary new image was based on emotional rather than rational assessment, an affective response rather than a cognitive understanding of the implications of the atomic bomb. From the outset, descriptions of detonations focused on the impressive mushroom cloud and were filled with theological references, not empirical data. Even the scientists who built the first atomic bomb responded to the power of their own creation with a decided lack of professional detachment. Thomas Farrell, upon witnessing the Trinity test, wrote that the blast "warned of doomsday and made us feel we puny things were blasphemous to dare tamper with the forces heretofore reserved for the Almighty."[22] Robert Oppenheimer recalled being reminded of an ancient Hindu verse from the *Bhagavad-Gita:* "like the splendor of the Mighty One . . . I am become death, the shatterer of worlds."[23] Similarly, William Laurence, whose assignment it was to record the event for history, wrote, "In that moment hung eternity. Time stood still. Space contracted to a pinpoint. It was as though the earth had opened and the skies split. One felt as though he had been privileged to witness the Birth of the World—to be present at the moment of creation when the Lord said: 'Let there be light.' "[24]

This emotional reaction was exploited throughout the following decade via official Atomic Energy Commission (AEC) press releases and public statements by political leaders that used similar imagery to prey on the public's fears. While Senator Joe McCarthy railed against the Communist threat, the Federal Civil Defense Administration (FCDA) distributed thousands of brochures and posters featuring pictures of the mushroom cloud and emphasized the need to be prepared for an attack. The FCDA also produced dozens of films shown in schools, churches, and social organizations that highlighted footage of the mushroom cloud from various detonations.[25]

The popular media assisted the government in disseminating and further institutionalizing the mushroom cloud as a symbol of U.S. "right and might." Widely read and highly respected publications ran articles on the new Atomic Age in which the mushroom cloud was invariably the centerpiece of every layout. When Harry Truman was named *Time* magazine's "Man of the Year" on December 21, 1945, his picture on the cover was dwarfed by a big mushroom cloud. Subsequently, dozens of newspapers and magazines including *Newsweek* ran photographic issues on the testing in Bikini, with dramatic shots of the mushroom cloud appearing on the covers.[26] *Life* magazine's picture of the week in 1951 was a shot of the mushroom cloud as the backdrop for Glitter Gulch in downtown Las Vegas.[27] A 1952 *New Yorker* article entitled "Our Far-Flung Correspondents: Blackjack and Flashes" featured photographs of the mushroom cloud, as did a 1953 article in *National Geographic* entitled "Nevada Learns to Live With the Atom" and the cover story in a 1955 issue of *Nevada Highways and Parks*.[28] Such noted journalists as Walter Cronkite, John Cameron Swayzee, and Bob Considine frequently reported on test shots from "News Nob" at the Nevada Test Site, always focusing on the visual effects of the blast with vivid descriptions of the mushroom cloud.[29]

Such media coverage not only facilitated the mass distribution of this emotion-laden symbol but also drew on the awesome beauty of the fireball to enhance the message. Spectacular imagery, poetic references, and colorful hyperbole focused the public's collective eye on the aesthetics of the mushroom cloud and glossed over the dangers that resulted from radioactive fallout. In one extreme case, Gunnery Sergeant Grant Powers, official combat artist, was commissioned to do a series of watercolors of mushroom clouds from shots detonated in the South Pacific, reproductions of which are now available on the Internet.[30] By hiding the truth behind artistically pleasing photographs, films, and officially sanctioned paintings, the government—with the help of the media—successfully diverted the public's attention from asking substantive questions about possible negative consequences and costs. Dazzled by atomic eye candy, citizens were virtually hypnotized into acceptance.

Finally, perhaps the most dramatic evidence of the mushroom cloud as political kitsch is found in the extent to which its stylized image invaded popular culture during the late 1940s and the 1950s. Just as New Year's postcards decorated with swastikas were big sellers in Nazi Germany, the mushroom cloud materialized on commercial objects and establishments across the United States. Intended to convey the message that a given product was hot, exciting, cutting-edge, and very American, the mushroom cloud was used to market everything from jawbreakers to underwear. Unlike Germany, with its official restriction on the use of the swastika, there were no legal limits on the mushroom cloud, and no article was declared too mundane for its imprimatur. The cloud appeared on album covers, postcards, and book jackets; it was featured in comic books and "price-smashing" sale notices; it lent its shape to hats, cakes, and neon signs; and it graced the shapely contours of beauty queens and Hollywood starlets. As Paul Boyer noted in his excellent study of American culture during this period, the mushroom cloud became "the quintessential visual symbol of the new era."[31]

Examples of the symbol's pervasiveness abound. The Atomic Record Company labeled its platters with a mushroom cloud, and the earliest album to feature the cloud on its dust jacket was a Count Basie recording, "$E=MC^2$."

6.2 1952 postcard of Pioneer Club in downtown Las Vegas with mushroom cloud.

The cover of an October 1946 *Action Comic* featured Superman photographing an atomic blast as he hovers near a giant mushroom cloud. Atomic Fireballs, the candy with "red hot flavor," were easily recognized by the red mushroom cloud on their yellow box. A publicity still from the MGM movie *The Beginning or the End* depicted four actors gazing to the future with a mushroom cloud looming in the background.

The Atomic Café in Los Angeles was known for its neon sign in the shape of a mushroom cloud, as was Atomic Liquors in Las Vegas. Best-selling postcards from Las Vegas depicted shots of Glitter Gulch with Vegas Vic in the foreground and a mushroom cloud in the distance. An official photograph of Vice Admiral Spike Blandy celebrating the success of the Bikini tests showed him with his wife cutting a mushroom cloud–shaped angel food cake. Meanwhile, in Las Vegas, Miss Atomic Bomb beauty pageant contestants wore fluffy white mushroom clouds pinned to the front of their bathing suits; and Gee Gee, hairstylist at the Flamingo, pulled women's hair over a wire frame shaped like a mushroom cloud and sprinkled it with silver glitter for that special-occasion "do." The Clark County seal featured a mushroom cloud, as did the cover of the Las Vegas phone book and the 1953 Las Vegas High School yearbook. Walt Disney produced a book for children on atomic power in which the mushroom cloud transmorphs into a benevolent genie, and a celebrity in the annual St.

George homecoming parade was Our Little Miss A-Bomb dre
lines shaped like a mushroom cloud. Even retailers used atomic in
pictures of mushroom clouds to advertise "atom-smashing sales prices."

Such permutations of the mushroom cloud in American popular cultu
like Friedlander's observations on Nazi kitsch, served to create a common
sensibility, a kind of harmony among the majority that fostered respect for the
established order. By taking a frightening phenomenon and making it familiar,
acceptable, nonthreatening, beautiful, and in some cases even desirable, the
mushroom cloud ingrained itself in the American psyche. Much like whistling
in the dark, it helped us to be unafraid and it shored up our confidence during
those highly uncertain times. Accordingly, it epitomizes political or uplifting
kitsch.

TRANSITION PERIOD

When testing moved underground in 1963 following ratification of the Limited Test Ban Treaty, it was a classic case of "out of sight, out of mind." Gone
was the ubiquitous mushroom cloud from the horizon; détente replaced the
international tensions of the previous decade; and the media turned their attention to other dramatic visuals such as race riots in Watts, napalm bombings
in Vietnam, and antics of the scantily clad flower generation. No longer a
desirable image deployed by the AEC, the mushroom cloud soon faded from
the American political and cultural scene. What had once been the generally
accepted symbol of everything good about America and simultaneously evil
about the Soviet Union was quickly abandoned by the U.S. government as it
sought to erase the public's memory of the dangerous aboveground testing
program.

For around twenty years the mushroom cloud virtually disappeared from
the visual vernacular. It reemerged only sporadically as a symbol of protest
within rather limited circles of the antinuke movement. A powerful and familiar image, the mushroom cloud appeared in protest literature, on antinuke T-
shirts and bumper stickers, and in several antiwar movies including the black
satire *Dr. Strangelove* (1964) and *On the Beach* (1959), based on Neville Shute's
classic novel. It also graced several record covers, among the most notable of
which were Jefferson Airplane's 1968 album *Crown of Creation* and *No Nukes*
produced by Electra Records in 1979, featuring protest songs by Jackson Browne,
James Taylor, and Bruce Springsteen. An unintended consequence of this counterculture deployment was the further kitschification of the mushroom cloud.
By disseminating the same political symbol, albeit with a different slant, the
unwitting protesters assisted the government in trivializing the dangers of the

...miliar and more established as an icon of main-

...M CLOUD AS NOSTALGIC KITSCH

...accelerating in the 1990s, the mushroom cloud ...ular culture as a powerful symbol. But unlike the ...tely promoted by the U.S. government, it resurfaced ...ste Olalquiaga calls "nostalgic kitsch"—a "cultural fossil" that ... ost golden moment, real or imaginary. Such objects reflect one's memory of a utopian situation that may never have existed but that over time has been extremely glorified. They conjure up a past "whose strength lies in its lack of immediate contingency, that is, in keeping the distance of abstraction." In other words, they eliminate the present to retain an "untouchable past." Accordingly, nostalgic kitsch evokes memories to dispel feelings of loss and rootlessness and fosters a sense of the past that provides continuity, belonging, and tradition.[33] This is clearly the case with the mushroom cloud, which in the decade prior to the terrorist attacks on September 11, 2001, had already become a symbol of simpler, better times—times when we knew who the enemy was; when we could trust our government; when our children were not on drugs, our schools were safe, and our heroes were not supermodels and rock stars.

Several factors account for the revival of the mushroom cloud as nostalgic kitsch. The release of *Atomic Café* (1982), an award-winning film intended to illustrate the naïveté of the American public during the early years of the Cold War, inadvertently contributed to the reemergence of "atomabilia." A collage of news clips and excerpts from old military training and civil defense films, the documentary reintroduced the audience to the now obviously pernicious public relations campaign employed by the government to build support for the arms race. Indeed, viewers were shocked initially at how foolish Americans must have been to believe such absurd claims, but they soon caught themselves smiling as they watched an animated Burt the Turtle sing and dance to "Duck and Cover." Other scenes, such as an interview with atomic soldiers attempting to mask their fear with false bravado and a father explaining to his children when it will be safe to leave the fallout shelter, evoked a sense of poignancy, which can be a first step toward nostalgia. The sound track, also released separately as an album, further reinforced this sentimentality with original cuts of atomic songs from the 1940s and 1950s, including "When the Atomic Bomb Fell" (1946) by Karl Davis and Harty Taylor and "Jesus Hits Like an Atom Bomb" (1950) by Lowell Blanchard and the Valley Trio.[37]

110

Second, the incredible transformation of the international political scene and the end of the Cold War brought a temporary euphoria to the American public. Coupled with a moratorium on nuclear weapons testing and nuclear arms reduction agreements, the demise of the Soviet Union allowed the U.S. citizenry to issue a collective sigh of relief.[34] As the likelihood of actually needing to use the bomb became more remote, the tendency to view it benignly in retrospect became more acceptable.

The passage of federal legislation compensating atomic victims for illnesses suffered as a result of exposure to radioactive fallout further contributed to this softening of feelings toward the bomb. The compensation program covered atomic soldiers, downwinders, nuclear workers, and uranium miners. This long overdue action both assuaged the nation's guilt and eliminated considerable public opposition to old A-bomb testing policies.[35] Landmark anniversaries celebrated during this period also fostered a nostalgic look at the nation's atomic past—the fiftieth anniversary of Pearl Harbor, D-Day, Trinity, and Hiroshima, for example. Not only did these events get extensive press coverage, complete with personal accounts and stories of American heroism, but they were supplemented by a barrage of World War II documentaries that ran on the popular television cable network, the History Channel. As we relished our victory in the Cold War, we were frequently reminded of our victory over fascism, which ultimately came with our dropping the A-bomb.

In response to this general nostalgic mood, Madison Avenue's advertising promotions throughout the last decade of the millennium drew heavily from styles and themes of the 1950s. As Breck Eisner, who directed Burger King's 45th anniversary spot featuring Shaquille O'Neal entering a Burger King in the 1950s, put it, "There's a certain comfort zone here."[36] Martinis, fur coats, and imported cigars—all artifacts from a bygone era of American greatness— once again became desirable articles for middle-class consumption. Vintage fashions and retro furniture fueled a cultural willingness among Americans to reflect upon, reminisce about, and subconsciously gloss over any offensive aspects of a mythical Golden Age.

In the wake of these developments, the mushroom cloud proliferated on a number of fronts. At the movies there was a renewed fascination with stories set against an atomic background; unlike the earlier sci-fi films—a genre whose origin many attribute to the atomic bomb—these were realistic dramas that used sets, costumes, and footage of mushroom clouds to evoke nostalgic images of the 1950s. *Desert Bloom* (1986), for example, is the coming-of-age story of a young woman in 1950s' Las Vegas whose loss of innocence parallels that of the nation as both watch the mushroom cloud on the horizon. *Fat Man and Little*

Boy (1989), starring Paul Newman as General Leslie Groves, is a fairly accurate accounting of the Manhattan Project; and *Night Breaker* (1989) unfolds as a flashback narrated by Martin Sheen, an atomic soldier who participated in war games at the Nevada Test Site. *Mulholland Falls* (1996) is a detective story in which Nick Nolte discovers that protection of radiation secrets at the Nevada Test Site is a motive for murder, and *Blue Sky* (1994) features Jessica Lange as a lonely wife in search of the truth about her husband's involvement in the testing program. The comedy *Blast From the Past* (1989), with Brendan Fraser and Sissy Spacek, is the story of a young man who emerges after spending his entire thirty-five years in a fallout shelter; the attitudes and styles portrayed in this time-warp presentation evoke memories of simpler times.

During the same period, television viewers were also exposed to several programs about the origin of the atomic bomb, in addition to those on the History Channel. The PBS docudrama *Day One* (1989)—based on the book by Peter Wyden and starring Brian Dennehy as General Groves—offered a less theatrical, more realistic look at the Manhattan Project than its big-screen counterpart. *Trinity and Beyond* (1995), produced by Peter Kuran—the animator for *Star Wars*—aired on the Discovery Channel; this ninety-five-minute documentary, narrated by William Shatner of *Star Trek* fame, included previously classified film stock of atomic blasts only recently released by the Department of Energy (DOE).[38]

Novelists, too, began to look back to the early days of atomic testing for plot lines. Martin Cruz Smith's spy novel *Stallion Gate* (1986) and Joseph Kanon's provocative murder mystery *Los Alamos* (1997), both set in New Mexico during the Manhattan Project days, became best-sellers. Critics heaped praise on both authors for their splendid blend of fact and fiction in a way that "brings this portentous page of history to vivid life." Pulitzer Prize–winning author Robert Olen Butler also used Los Alamos as a backdrop for his novel *Countrymen of Bones* (1983), about an archaeologist on a dig in the Jornada del Muerto mountains of New Mexico who becomes involved with characters—real and fictional—from the Trinity Test operations.[39]

These films and novels not only drew upon romanticized images from the past (clothes, cars, music), but they also projected a sense of excitement and intrigue that is appealing to the viewer and reader. They all included atomic blasts, but at the same time they were believable stories about ordinary people, not fantasies about incredible shrinking men or the end of the world. Such stylistic maneuvers helped create a sentimentalized myth about this period in history and thus reinforced the transition of the mushroom cloud, as a symbol of those times, into nostalgic kitsch.

The publication of nonfiction memoirs further contributed to, and is reflective of, this shifting attitude toward the early A-bomb. Several annotated picture albums from Manhattan Project days were released during the 1990s as "coffee-table" books. *Picturing the Bomb: Photographs From the Secret World of the Manhattan Project* (1995) by Rachel Fermi and Esther Sumra—the former the granddaughter of the noted scientist Enrico Fermi—is a personal scrapbook from her days as a child living in Los Alamos, as are Katrina Mason's *Children of Los Alamos: An Oral History of the Town Where the Atomic Age Began* (1995) and Peter Bacon Hales's *Atomic Spaces: Living on the Manhattan Project* (1997).[40]

The art world also witnessed a return of the mushroom cloud. Peter Goin's collection of photographs, *Nuclear Landscapes* (1991), shot with DOE permission at the Nevada Test Site, conjures up memories of the old Civil Defense tests in which "doom towns" were destroyed by atomic blasts.[41] "The Body of a House," an exhibit by Robert Beckmann, is a dramatic series of eight large-scale, iodine-colored paintings that surround the viewer with a millisecond visualization of a domestic dwelling destroyed by an atomic bomb. Describing the exhibit, Beckmann elaborates: "[T]he imagery is familiar to anyone who had grown up in the 50's ... the photos depicted a two-story farmhouse being destroyed by an above ground atomic bomb. As a child, that house had been my own home destroyed."[42] Although the text of Carole Gallagher's photographic essay *American Ground Zero: The Secret Nuclear War* (1993) is more overtly anti-government, her many pictures of individuals like Ken Case, the "Atomic Cowboy," also played on sentimentality.[43]

Taking a different but no less nostalgic approach, Bruce McCall's sketches for "The Last Dream-o-Rama" appearing in the *New Yorker* included fantasy cars from the 1950s that "go soaring into a futuristic empyrean of pop-up, push-button, retractable, multihued wonder, mirroring the optimism of a nation that now had the H-bomb, cinerama, and chlorophyll chewing gum." One such vehicle is the "Armageddon MK1," pictured beneath a mushroom cloud and described thus: "What better symbolized the American way than a top-down roadster with a foot-thick radiation shield and enough canned bologna in the back seat fallout shelter to feed the whole gang?"[44]

Other popular magazines reinforced this nostalgia. *Newsweek* devoted almost an entire issue to the bomb on its fortieth anniversary, *Time* featured a cover photo of a mushroom cloud rising over Hiroshima on the same date, and *People* magazine featured an interview with photographs of an unapologetic pilot Paul Tibbets fifty-five years after Hiroshima.[45] *Historic Preservation* ran a story "Echoes of the Cold War," with photographs from atmospheric blasts at the Nevada Test Site.[46] Similarly, *Archaeology* included an essay entitled "Proving

Ground of the Nuclear Age," in which the authors offer photos and vivid descriptions of the mangled towers, bridges, and hangars at the Nevada Test Site, concluding, "Our instincts lead us to believe that these artifacts of the Cold War are historically significant and need to be studied. Can anyone honestly call them non-archaeological?"[47]

An offshoot of this renewed public fascination with the early days of the Atomic Age, which further illustrates the kitschification of the mushroom cloud, was the growing promotion of "atomic tourism." "The Bureau of Atomic Tourism," a website graded A by *Entertainment Weekly* and selected as one of twenty "web gems" by the *Wall Street Journal,* is "dedicated to the promotion of tourist locations around the world that have either been the site of atomic explosions, display exhibits on the development of atomic devices, or contain vehicles that were designed to deliver atomic weapons." One can click for more information on such places as the Los Alamos County Historical Museum, where tourists can visit exhibits of items from the Manhattan Project and a gift shop that sells "Remember When?" pictorial calendars and earrings shaped like "Fat Man" and "Little Boy" as souvenirs.[48]

Meanwhile, the Travel Channel aired a special on tours of the Nevada Test Site that featured shots of certain structures shown on television for the first time. *Conde Nast Traveler* provided its readers with information on tours to Bikini Atoll, where adventurous scuba divers can explore the wrecks of warships sunk during atomic testing maneuvers: "A week on the island, including eleven decompression dives and a glow-in-the-dark souvenir (just kidding), is $2750."[49] And AAA's *Via* magazine ran a short article, "Testing, Testing . . . One, Two, Ka-boom!" containing details on how to book tours for the Nevada Test Site where "hundreds of huge saucerlike indentations dot the landscape."[50]

Las Vegas Life, a widely distributed promotional magazine, included a feature story, "Scenes From my Vacation, or How I Learned to Stop Worrying and Have a Blast Touring the Hot Spots of Cold War Science," by Stephen Fried. Borrowing his subtitle from the movie *Dr. Strangelove,* Fried takes the reader "through the scientific Americana of the great Southwest," stopping at Los Alamos, VLA antenna, Roswell, the Biosphere, and the Nevada Test Site. He concludes with the question, "Who needs pseudoscience when the real stuff is so damn dramatic?"[51] A shorter piece in the same magazine by Los Angeles–based author William Fox is a rather tongue-in-cheek proposal to turn the Nevada Test Site into a theme park. In "Blast From the Past," Fox argues that the test site would make a "hot" tourist attraction and, like Fried, ends with a question: "If other states direct visitors to Civil War sites . . . why would we ignore a living site that demonstrates the invention of the biggest gamble of all?"[52] Next door, *Around Albuquerque,* a slick tourist magazine found in hotels across New Mexico, included the story "A Pilgrimage to Trinity Site," complete with details on how to reach ground zero and what to wear for trekking around the site on the two days each year when it is open to the public. Come and stand "where, at man's command, the atom first turned itself inside out," the article beckons.[53] Whether serious or humorous, these various tourist promotions evoked nostalgic images and inevitably were accompanied by photos or artistic renditions of the mushroom cloud.

Finally, the return of the mushroom cloud has sparked a wave of atomic consumerism as shoppers seek to collect memorabilia from the era of atmospheric testing. One can purchase atomic comics, stamps, posters, photographs, and apparel. Also available are Warheads candy, Atomic Fireballs, a latex mask of the Simpsons' Radioactive Man, an Adam Bomb (one of the Garbage Pail kids) key ring, and a Nuclear War Card Game—"a comical cataclysmic card game" that should be played by "anyone who ever had to participate in a 'civil defense drill' by hiding under his or her desk in grade school, or ever had a bomb shelter in the backyard."[54]

Museums have also focused on our atomic heritage. In fall 2000 an exhibition at the University of Iowa library, "The Fifties: From Atomic Power to American Pie," deployed memorabilia from the decade to illustrate the "incongruities between the stereotype and realities of American life in mid-century."[55] The Brooklyn Museum of Art organized a touring exhibit that opened in fall 2001 entitled "Vital Forms: American Art and Design in the Atomic Age, 1940–1960." Among the featured items were curvy mushroom cloud–like furniture pieces from the 1950s that were rejected a decade later as too tacky or kitschy but are considered trendy today, as evidenced by the decor at many upscale restaurants including the neighborhood Starbucks. An article on the exhibit in *Smithsonian* referred to the decorative arts of this period as "bouncing to the detonation of exploding atoms."[56] Similarly, in 2002 the University Art Museum at the University of California, Santa Barbara, opened "Nuclear Families: The Home Fallout Shelter Movement in California, 1959–1969," an exhibition that looked at the societal, artistic, and architectural contexts of bomb shelters.[57]

A new web site devoted to atomic popular culture called www.conelrad.com has also appeared. Reviewed in the *New York Times,* the site "promises an overview and a thrillingly creepy look at America's postwar atomic culture."[58] As described in *USA Today,* the site, which has no particular political agenda, is a "stunning, sassy look" at atomic culture for those "feeling nostalgic for the Cold War" and offers "a way to explain 'duck and cover' to your children without sounding ridiculous."[59]

THE MUSHROOM CLOUD RETURNS TO GLITTER GULCH

Nowhere was the reappearance of the mushroom cloud more evident than in Las Vegas. This is not surprising given the nature of Las Vegas culture, which is based largely on kitsch; the political and economic impact of the test site on southern Nevada over the years; and the ongoing support for the test site expressed even today by many political leaders as well as local residents. Another factor contributing to the revival of the mushroom cloud as a symbol of Las Vegas, alongside showgirls and roulette wheels, may be the subconscious need to remind the rest of the country that Nevada has already done its part for national defense and therefore does not deserve to have a high-level nuclear waste dump imposed on the state against its will.

Finally and perhaps most significant, the celebration of the Nevada Test Site's fiftieth anniversary and the recent creation of the Nevada Test Site Historical Foundation, with its goal of building a museum and research center, propelled the mushroom cloud back to center stage in Nevada. Brochures for the foundation feature pictures of test shots, and its logo is a stylized orange cloud against a blue background that appears not only on the official stationery and newsletter but on articles for sale at its visitor center—including hats, T-shirts, coffee mugs, and lapel pins. Also available are commemorative calendars, photographs of mushroom clouds from various detonations, declassified videos of shots, and postcard reproductions of fireballs from throughout the 1950s. Upon its opening, a full-page newspaper story labeled the center "a museum with a kick."[60]

Currently, this "atomic shop" is a one-room store in an outlying DOE building, but its future site will be a $10.9 million facility located on the campus of the Desert Research Institute in Las Vegas. It will house old AEC records from the days of atmospheric testing; a museum sanctioned by the Smithsonian, exhibiting memorabilia from the Cold War era; and a conference center. The groundbreaking for the new facility coincided with the fiftieth anniversary of the Nevada Test Site, and appropriately, the event's program bore the foundation's familiar mushroom cloud logo. Besides local dignitaries, the event was attended by Nevada's U.S. senators, the director of the Smithsonian Institution's National Program Office, and the administrator of the National Nuclear Security Administration. Following the speeches, dignitaries ignited little A-bombs from which spewed smoke and silver confetti, creating a great visual that ran on all the local television stations and in the newspapers. "With miniature mushroom clouds rising behind them, Nevada politicians applaud fireworks . . . to mark 50th anniversary of the Nevada Test Site," read one caption.[61]

Site Lines, a DOE publication distributed to all test site employees and other interested parties throughout Nevada, ran a yearlong series entitled "50

Years at the NTS." It focused on "the events, places, and people" associated with the anniversary and featured old photographs and personal memoirs. "News Nob," the foundation's newsletter, ran numerous stories reminiscing about the old days of atmospheric testing. And to commemorate the anniversary of President Truman's announcement of his decision to begin "blowing up bombs in our backyard," the Las Vegas *Review Journal*—the largest newspaper in the state— kicked off a three-part series "The Test of Time." The first installment began with a full-page color shot of the mushroom cloud from Climax, a test conducted on June 4, 1953.[62]

Local merchants and advertisers capitalized on the revitalized mushroom cloud as well. The Stratosphere Tower ran an ad for "Vintage Vegas Nights" that used a reprint of the Miss Atomic Bomb beauty pageant winner to lure potential players.[63] An old atomic blast postcard hangs among the framed memorabilia on the walls of the popular seafood restaurant McCormick and Schmick. Ascentra, a professional health service, emphasized its virtues as a home-based company by using a picture of a mushroom cloud along with the message "Nevada welcomed prostitutes, gamblers, and atomic bombs. Let's draw the line with workers' compensation companies."[64] Nevada State Bank, in a half-page advertisement, asked the reader in script below a giant mushroom cloud, "Just waiting for the fallout? Don't panic."[65] New Line Cinema sponsored a swing dance competition at the Boulevard Mall in Las Vegas billed as "The 'Blast From the Past' Atomic Swing Thing." And Bechtel's brochure on the many services available at the new and improved test site includes a color photograph of a fireball and a mushroom cloud.

The Las Vegas high-culture scene also responded to the revived symbol with enthusiasm. *Neon,* the magazine of the Nevada Arts Council, ran a special edition with Miss Atom Bomb's picture on the cover, several photographs of mushroom clouds, and three short essays on Nevada's atomic past.[66] The Contemporary Arts Collective sponsored a fashion show fundraiser entitled "Hot, Hot, Haute! The Atomic Lounge." The accompanying program invited guests to "join us for a radiant evening" and included an enticing picture of a mushroom cloud. The Nevada Humanities Committee sponsored a lecture series on "Nevada in the Nuclear Age" with one of Peter Goin's photographs from the test site as its signature poster. And the University of Nevada Press published a new edition of *Bombs in the Backyard* with an eerie green paperback cover highlighted by the silhouette of a mushroom cloud.[67]

One last element of nostalgic kitsch worthy of note brings us full circle to where we began with the mushroom cloud as political kitsch because it is not only sanctioned but also produced by the government itself. It is an official

6.3 Miss Atom Bomb. Neon: Artcetera from Nevada Arts Council *(Spring-Summer 1999), Las Vegas News Bureau.*

6.4 Nevada Test Site license plate. Author's collection.

atomic license plate commemorating the role of the Nevada Test Site. From the fee for each plate sold, twenty-five dollars will go to the foundation to support its museum. The actual design of the plate was chosen in a competition won by Carson City resident Richard Bibbero. Selected over thirty other entries, it depicts a mushroom cloud flanked by the nuclear logo and Einstein's formula, $e=mc^2$.[68] Introduced in the 2001 legislature by Senator Dina Titus, the plate received considerable bipartisan support and was described by local television commentator George Knapp: "[T]he plates will rock. No sissy flowers or waterfall or scenery for us, like on other states' plates. We're talking the big one. The A-bomb. Serious firepower. Suffice it to say, our plate will kick sand in the face of any other plates on the road."[69]

CONCLUSION

Just as the mushroom cloud was settling down on the knickknack shelf of America's past, international events dramatically threatened its "cultural fossil" status. After September 11, 2001, peace was shattered, and fear was reinstated as the prevailing national emotion. Laughing at ourselves and our picturesque atomic past no longer seemed appropriate. Terrorist leader Osama Bin Laden's possible development of nuclear weapons, together with the India-Pakistan nuclear standoff, suddenly made the bomb real again. Likewise, President George W. Bush's 2002 State of the Union Address, with its focus on the "axis of evil" and its weapons of mass destruction; his push for a nuclear defense shield; his withdrawal from the 1972 Anti-Ballistic Missile Treaty with Russia;

and his directive to reduce the lag time before testing can resume in Nevada from two years to one all presage a return to Cold War–like nuclear policies.

The question now becomes what role the mushroom cloud will play in shaping America's mood as we enter the twenty-first century. Will it be exploited anew by the current political regime, or has it become so trivialized as to be no longer useful as a political symbol, replaced perhaps by a wanted poster of Bin Laden or a shot of the New York skyline without the Twin Towers? Will it remain on the horizon as a nostalgic icon reminding us of safer times when we could identify, find, and destroy the enemy? Will opponents of the administration's policy take it up once again as a symbol of protest? Will it fall from favor in Nevada as the nuke dump becomes a more imminent threat? Or will the mushroom cloud disappear because it is no longer relevant in a world of suicide bombers and suitcase nukes? Regardless of its short-term fate, however, I advise you to hang on to your fireball postcards and your "Fat Man" earrings; they could bring a good price someday at a flea market sale or earn you a tax deduction if you donate them to an atomic museum.

NOTES

I thank Hazel Wong, Stephanie Murphy, Jay Coughtry, and Mark Nash for their valuable assistance on this research project.

1. In order of quote: Herman Broch, "Notes on the Problem of Kitsch," from the article "Evil in the System of Values of Art," *Neue Rundschau* (August 1933), in *Kitsch, the World of Bad Taste,* ed. Gillo Darfles (New York: Universe, 1969), 68–76; Theodor W. Adorno, *Asthetische Theorie* (Frankfurt: Surkamp, 1970), 355; Matei Calinescu, *Five Faces of Modernity* (Durham: Duke University Press, 1987), 229; Celeste Olalquiaga, *The Artificial Kingdom* (New York: Pantheon, 1998), 28; Milan Kundera, *The Unbearable Lightness of Being* (New York: Harper and Row, 1984), 248.

2. *Jacobelli v. Ohio,* 378 U.S. 184 (1964).

3. Calinescu, *Five Faces,* 234–235.

4. Broch, "Notes on the Problem of Kitsch."

5. Clement Greenberg, "Avant-Garde and Kitsch," *Partisan Review* 6 (Fall 1939): 3–21.

6. Harold Rosenberg, *The Tradition of the New,* 2nd ed. (New York: McGraw-Hill, 1965), 268.

7. Hilton Kramer, "New Art of the 70s in Chicago: Visual Bluster and Camp Sensibility," *New York Times,* July 14, 1974.

8. Roger Scruton, "Kitsch and the Modern Predicament," *Urbanites* 9 (Winter 1999): 3.

9. Robert Nelson, "Deconstructing Kitsch," *The Age,* March 15, 2000: 1.

10. Theodor W. Adorno, "On Popular Music," *Studies in Philosophy and Social Science* 9 (1941): 17–48.

11. Dwight MacDonald, "A Theory of Mass Culture," in *Mass Culture,* ed. Bernard Rosenberg and D. M. White (New York: Free Press, 1964), 59–73; Leo Lowenthal, *Literature, Popular Culture, and Society* (Englewood Cliffs, NJ: Pacific, 1961).

12. Calinescu, *Five Faces.*

13. Jenny Sharp, "It's New, It's Different, It's Been Here All the Time," *Ark 41* (London: Royal College of Art, 1967), 24–25; Susan Sontag, "Notes on Camp," in Sontag, *Against Interpretation* (New York: Farrar, Straus and Geroux, 1966), 288.

14. Kundera, *Unbearable Lightness of Being,* 250.

15. Saul Friedlander, *Reflections of Nazism: An Essay on Kitsch and Death* (New York: Harper and Row, 1982).

16. Saul Friedlander, "Preface to a Symposium: Kitsch and the Apocalyptic Imagination," *Salmagundi* 85, 8 (1990): 201–206.

17. "On Kitsch: A Symposium," *Salmagundi* 85, 8 (1990): 227–231.

18. Murray Edelman, *From Art to Politics* (Chicago: University of Chicago Press, 1995).

19. Catherine Lugg, *Kitsch: From Education to Public Policy* (New York: Falmer, 1999), 118.

20. Ibid., 3–8.

21. F. L. Campbell, "Science on the March," *Scientific Monthly* (September 1945): 234.

22. John Savage and Barbara Storms, *Reach to the Unknown* (Los Alamos, NM: Atomic Energy Commission, 1965), 27.

23. Lansing Lamont, *Day of Trinity* (Garden City, NY: Doubleday, 1948), 235.

24. William L. Laurence, *Dawn Over Zero* (New York: Knopf, 1946), 237.

25. A. Costandina Titus, *Bombs in the Backyard,* 2nd ed. (Reno: University of Nevada Press, 2001), 70–85.

26. *Newsweek,* July 8, 1946.

27. *Life,* November 12, 1951, 37.

28. Daniel Lang, "Our Far-Flung Correspondents: Blackjack and Flashes," *New Yorker,* September 20, 1952, 90–99; Samuel Matthews, "Nevada Learns to Live With the Atom," *National Geographic* (June 1953): 839–850; "Operation 'Doom Town,' " *Nevada Highways and Parks* 13 (June–December 1955): 1–17.

29. Michael Uhl and Tod Ensign, *G.I. Guinea Pigs* (New York: Wideview, 1980), 76–77, 83.

30. www.history.navy.mil/ac/bikini.

31. Paul Boyer, *By the Bomb's Early Light,* 2nd ed. (Chapel Hill: University of North Carolina Press, 1994), 8.

32. Ibid; Titus, *Bombs in the Backyard*; A. Costandina Titus, "Cultural Fallout in the Atomic Age," in *History and Humanities,* ed. Francis Hartigan (Reno: University of Nevada Press, 1989), 121–136; A. Costandina Titus, "Back to Ground Zero: Old Footage Through New Lenses," *Journal of Popular Film and Television* (1983): 2–11; A. Costandina Titus, "Selling the Bomb: Hollywood and the Government Join Forces at Ground Zero," *Halcyon* (1985): 17–30; Titus and Jerry Simich, "From Atomic

Bomb Baby to Nuclear Funeral: Atomic Music Comes of Age, 1945–1990," *Popular Music and Society* (Winter 1990): 11–37; Michael Strader, "Kaleidoscopic Nuclear Images of the Fifties," *Journal of Popular Culture* (1986): 179–198; J. Fred McDonald, "The Cold War as Entertainment in Fifties Television," *Journal of Popular Film and Television* (1978): 3–31; Jack G. Shaheen, ed., *Nuclear War Films* (Carbondale: Southern Illinois University Press, 1978); Jerome Shapiro, *Atomic Bomb Cinema: The Apocalyptic Imagination on Film* (New York: Routledge, 2002).

33. Olalquiaga, *Artificial Kingdom*, 119–125.

34. Titus, *Bombs in the Backyard*, 145–147.

35. The Energy Employees Occupational Illness Compensation Program Act of 2000 (P.L. 106-398, Tittle 36); Radiation-Exposed Veteran Compensation Act of 1988 (P.L. 100-321); Radiation Exposure Compensation Act of 1990 (42 U.S.C. 2210).

36. Quoted in Roy White, "Why It's Cool to Troll Through Time," *Time*, April 8, 2002, 16.

37. *Atomic Café*, prod. and dir. Jayne Loader, Kevin Rafferty, and Pierre Rafferty, Archives Project, 1982.

38. Peter Wyden, *Day One: Before Hiroshima and After* (New York: Warner, 1984).

39. Martin Cruz Smith, *Stallion Gate* (New York: Random House, 1986); Joseph Kanon, *Los Alamos* (New York: Doubleday, 1997); J. D. Reed, *People,* vol. 47, issue 23 (June 16, 1997), 32; Robert Olen Butler, *Countrymen of Bones* (New York: Henry Holt, 1983).

40. Rachel Fermi and Esther Sumra, *Picturing the Bomb: Photographs From the Secret World of the Manhattan Project* (New York: Harry Abrams, 1995); Katrina Mason, *Children of Los Alamos: An Oral History of the Town Where the Atomic Age Began* (New York: Twain, 1995); Peter Bacon Hales, *Atomic Spaces: Living on the Manhattan Project* (Urbana: University of Illinois Press, 1997).

41. Peter Goin, *Nuclear Landscapes* (Baltimore: Johns Hopkins University Press, 1991).

42. Quoted in program for the exhibit at Amarillo Museum of Art, Amarillo, Texas, May–June 22, 1997.

43. Carole Gallagher, *American Ground Zero: The Secret Nuclear War* (Lunenburg, VT: Stinehour, 1993). Reflecting similar antigovernment sentiments, another genre of books that appeared during this period and often featured pictures of the mushroom cloud focused on the stories of various atomic victims' groups; see Titus, *Bombs in the Backyard*, 208–209, notes 21, 29, 30, 37.

44. Bruce McCall, "The Last Dream-o-Rama," *New Yorker,* August 6, 2001, 60–63.

45. P. Goldman, "Living With the Bomb," *Newsweek,* July 29, 1985, 28–50; R. Rosenblatt, "The Atomic Age," *Time,* July 29, 1985, 32–46; *People,* August 12, 2000, 89–90.

46. Allen Freeman, "Echoes of the Cold War," *Historic Preservation* (January–February 1994): 28–35.

47. William G. Johnson and Colleen Beck, "Proving Ground of the Nuclear Age," *Archaeology* (May–June 1995): 49.

48. www.atomictourist.com.

49. Cleo Kilbride, "Origins and Endings: Bikini," *Conde Nast Traveler* (July 2000): 118–119.

50. Margaret Lee, "Testing, Testing . . . One Two, Ka-Boom!" *Via* (July-August 2001): 28.

51. Stephen Fried, "Scenes From My Vacation, or How I Learned to Stop Worrying and Have a Blast Touring the Hot Spots of Cold War Science," *Las Vegas Life* (May 2001): 61–66.

52. William L. Fox, "Blast From the Past," *Las Vegas Life* (August 2000): 32.

53. "A Pilgrimage to Trinity Site," *Around Albuquerque* (Winter-Spring 2001): 28–29.

54. See, for example, funforalltoys.com.

55. "From Atomic Power to American Pie," October 2000–January 2001, www.lib.uiowa.edu/news/release/exhibit_atomic.html (February 20, 2001).

56. Doug Stewart, "Cheese Holes, Blobs, and Woggles," *Smithsonian* (February 2002): 48.

57. Jeannine Stein, "What Lies Beneath," *Los Angeles Times,* February 2, 2002.

58. Michael Pollak, "Eerie, Creepy Look at Cold War Culture," *New York Times,* September 23, 1999.

59. *USA Today,* February 14, 2002.

60. Las Vegas *Sun,* July 15, 2000.

61. Las Vegas *Review Journal,* December 19, 2000.

62. Las Vegas *Review Journal,* December 17, 2000.

63. Las Vegas *Review Journal,* February 2, 2000.

64. *Nevada Business Journal* (October 1999): 11.

65. Las Vegas *Sun,* May 5, 1996.

66. Phyllis Barber, "How I Got Cultured: A Nevada Memoir," 6–8, Andre Codrescu, "From Las Vegas," 12, and Michon Mackedon, "Speaking Atomic," 17–21, excerpts in *Neon: Artcetera From the Nevada Arts Council* (Spring-Summer 1999).

67. Titus, *Bombs in the Backyard.*

68. Las Vegas *Review Journal,* April 13, 2002.

69. Nevada Senate Bill 264, passed the Senate unanimously on April 24, 2001; defeated in Assembly on May 8; added as an amendment to Assembly Bill 643, which passed on May 30, 2001, 71st session. Also, George Knapp's "Street Talk," KLAS-TV, May 3, 2001.

CHAPTER SEVEN

Is This the Sum of Our Fears?

Nuclear Imagery in Post–Cold War Cinema

MICK BRODERICK

Today it all seems so naïve, so idealistic, a towering grand illusion. For one brief, shining decade—a dozen years, tops—we'd convinced ourselves that the thermonuclear shadow had receded, the doomsday clock had been set to "snooze," the threat of planetary suicide had vanished along with the Soviet Empire, apartheid and other cruel relics of the 20th century.

—Reed Johnson, "The Bomb Is Back,"
Los Angeles Times, June 18, 2002

When the *Los Angeles Times,* Hollywood's industry-town broadsheet, on four separate occasions within a couple of months devotes significant feature space to examining cinema's responses to nuclear fears, it's safe to assume something is happening in the zeitgeist.[1]

Like Johnson, *Times* film critic and movie historian Kenneth Turan was moved to contextualize a review of *The Sum of All Fears* with a lengthy missive on the cycles of nuclear fear and how movies have responded to that fear. Whereas feature writer Johnson teases out the ideology of such films, suggesting that their narratives have continued traditions of imagining apocalypse, Turan assesses the industry and audience mood as desperate to understand what a potential homeland nuclear attack might be like to witness, if only vicariously.

Most of these opinion pieces suggest that American cinema is once again returning to explore issues and themes that were somehow less apparent during the past decade, when the geopolitical and ideological battles between communism and capitalism attained closure in what Francis Fukuyama has described as "the end of history" and others regard as late capitalism or postmodernism. But *what* is it exactly that mainstream feature dramas have meant to eschew for the past ten or so years? A close analysis of what I have earlier defined as nuclear movies will suggest some surprises and perhaps contradictions in this recent journalistic trend spotting.[2]

Given the limited space available and the veritable dearth of relevant movies, it is necessary to gloss over many of the more prominent and perhaps less obvious directions this nuclear genre has adopted in the post–Cold War era. Hence, I will discuss a number of key films and some others about the periphery that have either continued the genre's motifs or been mutated in interesting ways. Among these deviations I will concentrate on the recent sociohistorical focus on the early 1960s (particularly the Cuban Crisis) as a cultural milieu; the deployment of nuclear weapons technology as a force of liberation, not destruction; and depictions of nuclear terrorism.[3] Other major directions of post–Cold War nuclear cinema that are, unfortunately, outside the scope of this analysis include the continued relevance of imagined postholocaust worlds[4] (e.g., *Hardware, Future Force* [1990], *Terminator 2: Judgment Day* [1991], *Neon City* [1992], *Return to Frogtown* [1993], *No Escape* [1994], *Waterworld* [1995], *Danger Zone* [1996], *The Postman* [1997], *Crazy Six* [1998], *Terminator 3: Rise of the Machines* [2003]) and movie remakes of Cold War films that alter the originals' nuclear context, or narrative "MacGuffin"[5] (e.g., *Twelve Monkeys* [1996], a supervirus, not holocaust; *Planet of the Apes* [2001], genetics rather than nuclear war; *The Time Machine* [2002], which deletes the 1966 atomic war; *Godzilla* [1998], spawned from French as opposed to U.S. nuclear tests; and *Spiderman* [2002], bitten by a genetically engineered, not a radioactive, arachnid[6]).

ENDING THE COLD WAR?

Most observers place the Cold War's dissolution somewhere between the tearing down of the Berlin Wall (November 1989) and the foiled coup against President Mikhail Gorbachev (August 1991) that witnessed the ascendancy of Boris Yeltsin alongside the corresponding transition from the Soviet Union to the Commonwealth of Independent States (early 1992). By conservatively taking 1989 as the key nodal point in the Cold War/post–Cold War chronology, it is possible to create a quantitative and qualitative taxonomy of films (approximately 500 international feature dramas from 1989 to 2002) that have continued to represent nuclear imagery and themes and to compare and contrast these films with the preceding (predominantly Cold War) genre of nuclear movies.

The other significant temporal boundary for this analysis is the international war on terrorism instigated by the United States and a coalition of mostly Western forces following the September 11, 2001, attacks on New York and Washington, D.C. The allied, though principally U.S.-led, assault on Taliban and Al-Qa'ida forces in Afghanistan represents a hot war, just as the previous decade's other international wars in the Gulf and Balkans were hot. Invoking a crusade against his Islamic terrorist foes and describing as an "axis of evil" the nation-states (Iraq, Iran, and North Korea) actively pursuing weapons of mass destruction, the rhetoric of George W. Bush and his administration closely resembles that of his 1980s' presidential predecessor, Ronald Reagan.[7] The parallels are stark. Apart from the widely perceived unfinished business of violently removing his father's nemesis, Saddam Hussein, from Iraq, George W. is following Reagan into space with a ballistic defense shield—a watered-down Star Wars Strategic Defense Initiative (SDI)—to deter "rogue states" from annihilating U.S. cities with intercontinental ballistic missiles (ICBMs) or intermediate-range ballistic missiles (IRBMs).[8]

Finally, one major temporal feature of this past decade has been its proximity to the new millennium and its passing. Many scholars have recognized the importance of millenarian and apocalyptic modes in which popular culture has traditionally entertained visions of the nuclear age.[9]

THE WINNING WEAPON

Perhaps the most significant change in nuclear cinema during the past decade has been the manner in which nuclear weapons are featured within the narratives and mise-en-scène of some post–Cold War films. During the 1980s nuclear weapons were most frequently depicted as the technology that would bring about a secular apocalypse in which manmade and man-used weapons of mass destruction could theoretically, in the worst-case scenario, erase the human species from the planet.[10]

Productions such as *World War III* (1980), *The Day After* (1983), *Testament* (1983), *Threads* (1984), *The Dead Zone* (1984), *Wargames* (1984), *One Night Stand* (1985), *Countdown to Looking Glass* (1986), *When the Wind Blows* (1987), and *Miracle Mile* (1988) depicted their holocausts (or the potential for them) as dependent upon the doctrine of Mutual Assured Destruction or, alternatively, preemptive strikes that would afford a qualitative, if pyrrhic, postnuclear "victory."

In most cases the catastrophic effects of a nuclear attack were presented if not graphically, then at least rhetorically and through overt narrative exposition.

Hence, nuclear weapons were constructed in these dramatic fictions as the malign agents of unimaginable destruction, the shatterer of worlds. Nuclear cinema and television of the 1980s mainly avoided scenarios whereby nuclear weapons were deployed to do anything other than deter the unthinkable or to embrace it preemptively or retaliate devastatingly against such preemption. Following the end of the Cold War, however, with the Reagan-Gorbachev baby steps in arms reduction eliminating an entire class of weapons via the Intermediate-Range Nuclear Forces Treaty, strategic arms reduction was back on the negotiating table in an effort to wind back the two superpowers' combined 50,000-plus nuclear weapons. Superficially at least, successive U.S. and Russian administrations have moved to bring about both bilateral and unilateral reductions in the strategic weapons arsenal, trimming the current active stockpile to approximately 16,400 (8,400 Russian and 8,000 U.S. weapons).[11] The ongoing arms cull, coupled with the 1999 Comprehensive Test Ban Treaty and the renewed Nuclear Non-proliferation Treaty, are significant international acts that appear to stabilize and ameliorate the global nuclear threat. However, despite the headline news, these major arms reductions treaties still require ratification. Similarly, since the threshold for inducing a Nuclear Winter is believed to be around 1,000 nuclear detonations, both superpowers will easily attain that sum even after the most stringent strategic cuts take place by 2012.[12]

Yet concerns remain. Prior to New Year's Day 2000, a global information technology (IT) campaign was initiated to prevent the "Y2K bug" from causing software problems in most operating systems around the world. Gravest concerns centered on former Soviet Union command and control systems because of the country's aging and outmoded nuclear deterrent, as well as the potential for Chernobyl-like meltdowns of archaic reactors if computer dates were compromised.[13] But the global Y2K countdown to catastrophe fizzled, and the technological prophets of doom responded predictably to the age-old manifestation of cognitive dissonance when such prophecies fail by retrospectively changing the date (to 02/02/02) or back-slapping each other for averting disaster with prudent warnings and billions spent on preventative measures.[14] Y2K is now relegated to the background noise of our collective cultural memory. It is amusing to speculate whether future scholars will regard this event as yet another manifestation of bogus millennial angst totally consistent with ancient chiliastic anxiety (Black Death, Antichrists, the Crusades, and similar disasters), regardless of the purported technological veracity identified by IT experts around the world.

If anticipated nuclear cataclysms inspired by Y2K signaled a deep cultural mistrust of computerized technology, symptomatic of our First World (post)modern malaise, then it is important to recall that several blockbuster movie entertainments only a few years earlier had celebrated nuclear weapons and associated technologies as *beneficent* forces, harnessed by humanity to liberate it from external threats—whether cosmic or alien. As in the first two *Alien* films (1981, 1986), nuclear obliteration provides the principal means of destroying the eponymous foes' outposts. In the first film the *Nostromo's* onboard thermonuclear self-destruct sequence is programmed to annihilate the extraterrestrial. In the sequel, the human colony (overrun by aliens) is vaporized by destroying the planet's massive fusion reactors. Similarly, *Total Recall* (1991) depicts a vast Martian nuclear-powered atmospheric generator as responsible for the ecological *renewal* of the planet and, by implication, of homo sapiens.[15]

Post–Cold War cinema continues this trope, but the stakes are presented as explicitly apocalyptic and not allegorical or metaphoric. Three of the biggest Hollywood films of the period (*Independence Day* [1995], *Deep Impact,* and *Armageddon* [both 1999]) all present narratives in which planetary devastation looms as imminent. In each film the use of nuclear weapons is crucial to the liberation of humanity and the eradication of the external threat.

Independence Day, or *ID4* as it was marketed internationally, ironically returns mass entertainment to the milieu of Cold War science fiction (SF). The film is replete with transtextual and intertextual references to popular culture, ranging from the contemporary opening diegetic music—REM's "It's the End of the World as We Know It (and I Feel Fine)"—the now clichéd establishment of an awesome spacecraft engulfing the entire frame and mise-en-scène (as in Lucas's *Star Wars*), through to Truman and Eisenhower–era SF cinema (*The Thing From Another World* [1951], *War of the Worlds* [1953], and *Earth Versus the Flying Saucers* [1956], to name a few).[16] The playful grafting of familiar generic elements to fashion a post–Cold War near future tale, with its youthful Gulf War fighter hero/president, resonates with Fredric Jameson's notion of nostalgia in postmodern cultural expression. But *ID4* is not merely an empty exercise in postmodern pastiche. The film builds on the earlier Cold War cinema and morphs (or mutates) it into a hybrid narrative that extends generic conventions through self-conscious repetition for a media-savvy or, alternatively, historically naive audience in the hope of satisfying both.[17]

The film varies the 1950s' film adaptation of *War of the Worlds* by replicating imagery of an apparently impenetrable alien shield that repels human aggression via some unknown force field. In both films, after successive conventional attacks fail, a nuclear strike is ordered. And whereas biological infection accidentally overpowers the 1950s Martians in keeping with the Wells novel, in *ID4* a computer virus infects the invading spacecraft long enough for a human "Trojan horse" attack to occur. In the 1995 film human ingenuity (software, programming, hacking) enables a clandestine sortie to infiltrate the mother ship and deliver a thermonuclear coup de grace. The aliens are ultimately defeated by the use of nuclear weapons, not the random bacteriological diversity of the earth's ecosphere.[18]

Along the way, however, *ID4* perhaps unconsciously betrays a subtext that gestures late-twentieth-century nuclear history. Produced and distributed for a summer 1995 release, the film situated itself among the controversial fiftieth anniversary dates surrounding the Trinity test and the Hiroshima/Nagasaki atomic bombings. The Smithsonian Institution's compromised *Enola Gay* exhibition provided further context for the film's highly anticipated reception. As such, the plot of *Independence Day*—the title itself connotes a host of American historical associations—can be read in part as providing a revisionist allegory of Pearl Harbor and Hiroshima. If the opening surprise attack against the United States references Roosevelt's "day of infamy," the corresponding concluding nuclear explosion provides a historical typology of the Hiroshima A-bombing. Similarly, foreign audiences may have been more attuned to the irony of Hollywood depicting the United States held hostage to a hostile Other that possesses an impenetrable defense shield that renders the domestic deterrent useless and provides the aggressor with impunity to attack with high-energy beam weapons.

Sound familiar? Throughout the late 1980s and to this day, successive U.S. administrations have embraced the technological fantasy that a nuclear defense shield, whether a Strategic Defense Initiative or George W. Bush's more modest National Missile Defense, would eliminate or greatly reduce the possibility of a successful nuclear attack against U.S. territory. That American popular culture was metaphorically reflecting this posture from the perspective of SDI opponents and antagonists remains somewhat curious.

So the (American) nuclear deterrent is afforded agency in *ID4*. It is the means by which human society (represented more or less exclusively by the United States) can overcome national, if not global, threats. No longer assigned to the role of Mutually Assured Destruction deterrent as relics of a Cold War past, these weapons are given utility in *Independence Day*—transforming from potentially malign, hyper-redundant (i.e., overkill), and static symbols of Cold War hegemony to benign, useful, and expendable technologies that can save the species, not destroy it.

Occasionally in the nuclear genre, two or more films enter production dealing with identical themes. Toward the end of the 1980s, for instance, a small wave of nuclear submarine films were produced that dealt with the perils of the technology and the hostile environment in which they operate when facing irrational and inexplicable forces (*The Abyss, The Rift, Deep Star Six, Leviathan, Full Fathom Five,* all released from 1989 to 1991).[19] In 1996 the comet Shoemaker-Levi was photographed plunging into Jupiter's atmosphere and gouging out earth-size–diameter impact zones across the gaseous planet's surface. It was a startling event that reignited debate about the need for scanning the solar system to locate threatening near-earth objects and to consider viable defenses against such scenarios.[20] The post–Cold War blockbuster entertainments *Deep Impact* (1998) and *Armageddon* (1988) both depict the earth imperiled by the threat of planetary impact as heavenly bodies approach (a comet and an asteroid, respectively). In each film nuclear weapons are the last resort available to prevent calamity when extinction is forecast on the scale of the late Jurassic era.[21]

Deep Impact concentrates on the endeavors of the executive branch of the government and the mass media in preparing for and managing the crisis in order to prevail, as well as portraying a nuclear-armed international space mission launched to deflect or partially disintegrate the comet. *Armageddon* centers its narrative on a motley crew of oil riggers sent to rendezvous with an approaching Texas-sized asteroid and place nuclear charges at its core in order to destroy it. Whereas *Deep Impact* takes its rhetorical narrative position with earnest and solemn aplomb, *Armageddon* superficially embraces comic cynicism to laugh off the apocalyptic threat (e.g., Steve Buscemi inanely riding a nuke in an ineffectual nod to *Dr. Strangelove* [1964]). Whereas *Deep Impact* frequently privileges middle-class American perspectives, with its dour black American president and affluent families embroiled in domestic turmoil, *Armageddon* sides with rugged individualism and jingoism and seemingly revels in the red-neck sensibility of its folk heroes as they save the world. Bruce Willis, for example, is introduced to the audience atop an oil rig contemptuously driving off volleys of golf balls from the elevated platform at a protesting Greenpeace vessel below him. The derision shown toward the environmentalists establishes the movie's popularist ethos: effete do-gooder ecologists won't save the planet, but square-jawed working stiffs literally oiling the wheels of big business will.

Both films, however, universalize the utility of nuclear weapons as the means of averting doomsday. The very title *Armageddon* evokes apocalyptic discourse, although somewhat erroneously since this biblical term connotes the location of the penultimate battle on earth between the forces of good and evil. *Deep Impact* elides such overt association, but apocalyptic rhetoric informs the narrative at key points—such as naming the spacecraft delivering its atomic cargo the *Messiah*. But like *Independence Day*, in these scenarios nuclear weapons alone are not sufficient to save humankind; it takes ingenuity and self-sacrifice (the "right stuff") to deliver the atomic blow in the right place and at the right time.[22]

NUCLEAR TERRORISM

A cinematic indicator of how "the more things change the less things change" can be found in a hilarious scene from *Austin Powers: International Man of Mystery* (1996), when the fiendish Dr. Evil is awakened from cryogenic suspension after thirty years. Before his lackeys and business associates Dr. Evil immediately proposes a number of diabolical schemes, only to be reluctantly informed by his underlings that decades of accrued corporate and political corruption have overtaken his no longer inventive master plans. With a resigned shrug Dr. Evil acquiesces:

> Oh, hell, let's just do what we always do. Let's hijack some nuclear weapon and hold the world hostage. [pause] Gentlemen, it's come to my attention that a breakaway Russian Republic called Kreplachistan will be transferring a nuclear warhead to the United Nations in a few days. Here's the plan. We get the warhead, and we hold the world ransom.

In *Austin Powers* this standard, if hackneyed, nuclear terrorist ploy for world domination (like those repeated in *Royce* [1994], *Broken Arrow* [1996], *Jackie Chan's First Strike* [1997], and *Hamilton* [1989], to name a mere few) becomes a source of comic ridicule and demonstrates that attitudes toward imagining terrorism in the Atomic Age have remained remarkably stable.[23]

The end of the Cold War has done nothing to ease such concerns, as an examination of Austin Powers's originary persona and genre urtext, James Bond, reveals. As a literary and cinematic cultural product of the Cold War spanning more than five decades, the character and contexts of 007 narratives are productive barometers for evaluating changing perceptions of nuclear terrorism. Bond more often than not represents opposing cultural and ideological values, becoming, as Tony Bennett and Janet Woollacott have suggested in *Bond and Beyond*, a "moving sign of the times"—particularly in terms of representing relations between East and West, the sexes, and colonialism and nationhood.[24]

Throughout the Cold War the ideological expression of Bond films was never static or monolithic and can be readily mapped against their historical alignment with (or deviation from) Cold War sentiment.[25] Just as earlier postwar serials and cliff-hangers encountered themes of nuclear terrorism (e.g., *Lost*

City of the Jungle [1946], *Black Widow* [1947]), the Bond mov
depicted the West as threatened by criminal masterminds, w
disaffected militarists pursuing either financial reward or glo
by employing some form of nuclear blackmail. As I have
strated, of all the Bond films to date, the vast majority of ʃ
technology as the rationale for 007's timely interventions.[26]

After dumping Timothy Dalton as his new post–Cold War Bond, longtime
007 producer Albert "Cubby" Broccoli cast Pierce Brosnan. There is some
irony and synergy in Brosnan taking on the role of the West's most invincible
secret agent. In a preceding role that suggests Brosnan has come full circle
while perhaps still remaining typecast, he also appeared in *The Fourth Protocol*
(1987) as a ruthless KGB assassin clandestinely assembling a nuclear bomb
smuggled into the United Kingdom (UK) and next to a North Atlantic Treaty
Organization airbase, triggered to explode during a peace rally and to thereby
bring about the collapse of the Western alliance.[27] Less known publicly is that
the environmentally conscious Brosnan, who performs pro bono in many public service advertisements, planned to use his appearance at a Paris premiere of
Goldeneye (1995) to "attack nuclear testing in the South Pacific" at a time
when France had unilaterally resumed such testing on the Polynesian atoll of
Mururoa.[28] The French defense minister wisely cancelled the film event.

Despite the apparent thaw in superpower tensions and the West's embrace
of China in globalized markets, nuclear terrorism themes have been maintained in post–Cold War Bond adventures. In *Tomorrow Never Dies* (1996) an
international media mogul sets about creating a nuclear war between China
and the United Kingdom (at a time when the UK was to relinquish sovereignty
over the colony of Hong Kong) to consolidate his monopoly interests in the
People's Republic. The scheme, inevitably foiled by Bond, is precipitated by
the sinking of a British warship with a private Stealth interceptor. Reflecting
China's emerging strategic and economic interests for the United States, the
movie's Central Intelligence Agency (CIA) operative states bluntly that Uncle
Sam will remain neutral in any such conflict, adding "we have no interest in
World War III unless *we* start it."

More recently, in *The World Is Not Enough* (1999) Bond is sent to several
former Soviet republics in pursuit of a local terrorist. A complex web of deceit
and subterfuge embroils 007 in a sophisticated gambit to steal a decommis-
sioned Russian nuclear warhead to sabotage a strategic oil pipeline. The warhead explodes, but since half of the plutonium has been secretly removed it is
subcritical. With the aid of a beautiful U.S. nuclear scientist employed to over-
see strategic arms dismantling, Bond discovers the remaining fissile material is

be inserted into the reactor of a commandeered Russian submarine, hidden in Istanbul.[29] The latest 007 venture, *Die Another Day* (2003), eschews the obvious association (one both the UK and the United States have been asserting) that North Korea is exporting nuclear weapons technology to other rogue states. The Bond movie depicts the Communist space weapon as capable of vaporizing any incoming nuclear missile that attempts to attack it. In this scenario, ironically, North Korea embodies the concern many nations have regarding the potential U.S. rationale for its own space defense shield, suspiciously regarding it as an *offensive* weapon—making it impervious to a first strike while undertaking its own unilateral actions internationally.

A frequent motif returned to in nuclear terrorism tales is the smuggling of a nuclear device (often in a briefcase, backpack, or suitcase) into the continental United States. As early as 1946, when Robert Oppenheimer was asked by a nervous Congress if an instrument could be made to detect atom bomb components being smuggled into the country, the Manhattan Project chief replied that one already existed—the screwdriver—to open every crate and container brought into every American port. These fantasies are nothing new, however, and date back to 1950s thrillers such as *Five Days to Noon* (1951), *The 49th Man* (1953), and *Port of Hell* (1955).

The much anticipated debut film from DreamWorks-SKG was *The Peacemaker* (1997), a taut political thriller that depicts a stolen nuclear weapon from the former Soviet Union about to be detonated in downtown Manhattan by Yugoslavian terrorists.[30] Although a nuclear scientist intelligence specialist and a special forces colonel save the city by removing enough of the bomb's high-explosive casing surrounding the plutonium core, it does indeed go off but fails to reach criticality. Instead of millions dead and buildings razed, only a New York church and its neighboring block are affected. Presumably peppered with aerosolized radionuclides, the two heroes emerge from the blast bruised and bloodied at the film's conclusion—ludicrously to be embraced and congratulated by the assembled police and fire brigades. However, what has escaped attention—particularly in light of current concerns regarding terrorists who without the know-how to manufacture a working nuke may adopt the more likely scenario of exploding "dirty" radiological weapons within U.S. cities—is that the contamination from such an event would be widespread and long lasting, costing the local economy billions. Hence, *The Peacemaker*'s subcritical explosion, although erroneously glossing the effects, may be unknowingly prophetic in its outcome.

Other more recent films have found alternative ways of deploying their suitcase bomb trope. Films such as *Big Trouble* (2001-2002) and *Bad Company*

(2002) provide comic or wisecracking characters to convey some discursive levity while relating their "unthinkable" plots. The former film depicts a couple of daft hoods smuggling a hidden nuke aboard a passenger jet, whereas the latter more conventionally follows a CIA sting operation to acquire a black-market warhead. Among the nuclear terrorist films released after 9/11, *The Sum of All Fears* (2002), based on the best-selling 1991 Tom Clancy novel, plays it straight and is deadly earnest. The fourth in a disparate espionage series involving CIA analyst Jack Ryan, it is the most detailed in its depiction of nuclear weapons, proliferation, terrorism, and post–Cold War strategic policy. Unlike the MacGuffin of many other nuclear terrorist films, *The Sum of All Fears* provides a sophisticated historical context and nuanced rendering of events prior to its penultimate catastrophe—a clandestine nuclear bomb detonated in Baltimore.

In the opening credit sequence, as a large bomb (as yet unidentified as atomic) is attached to an Israeli jet fighter's undercarriage, intertitles relate how at one crucial point during the 1973 Middle East war the Jewish state faced sudden defeat by Egyptian and Syrian forces. The jet is clearly an American-supplied F-4 Phantom; hence, the link between Israel's armaments and U.S. regional strategic interests is abundantly clear. Shortly after takeoff the plane is hit by a surface-to-air missile and crashes in the Golan Heights, where its single bomb remains buried and forgotten for nearly two decades. The bomb is ostensibly purchased on the black market for $50 million by a neo-Nazi consortium, and the film makes it clear that the device's fissionable plutonium was manufactured in the United States and covertly but officially "stolen" to conveniently make its way into the secret Israeli atomic arsenal.

The fact that a telltale radioactive signature obtained later from the Baltimore fallout enables defense analysts to bull's-eye its U.S. point of origin is a crucial plot point and one that ultimately leads to a rapid de-escalation of nuclear brinkmanship where the consequences for both superpowers are a catastrophic intercontinental exchange. The neo-Nazi plan is to obliterate America and Russia through nuclear entrapment, propelling the adversaries into rash decisions whereby both sides fear imminent preemptive attacks. With the anticipated decimation of the former Cold War foes, fascism will reemerge to become the principal unifying ideology and herald a return to global domination.

Perhaps the most impressive sequence in the film is the depiction of the nuclear detonation, which still manages to shock regardless of the precipitous narrative setup that makes it inevitable. The actual explosion—flash, blast, and heat—occurs within seconds but with impressive detail. The shock wave and concussion destroy a fleeing presidential motorcade and fell a helicopter carrying

CIA analyst Jack Ryan. The broiling computer-generated image mushroom cloud (seen twice) and closeups of monstrous advancing clouds of dust and debris instantly evoke flashbacks to TV news visions of the collapsing World Trade Center and the lower Manhattan skyline blanketed in billowing smoke.

Nevertheless, for all its initial frisson, *The Sum of All Fears* essentially downplays, if not avoids, the consequences of a small-kiloton explosion in an astrodome car park during a sellout football game. Considering the film's provocative title, there is no explicit *sum* of the Baltimore fatalities, let alone casualties.[31] The film eschews representation of the smoking crater the astrodome would have become and avoids mentioning the tens of thousands of spectators who would have been instantly vaporized from the explosion and the untold radiation deaths resulting from what would be a very dirty fission detonation and its corresponding local and downwind fallout. We do see an overcrowded hospital ward trying to cope with a few burn and blast injuries and some collateral damage closer to ground zero, where buildings are ablaze and the streetscapes in disarray. But this cinematic simulation is hardly the sum of all fears.

RETURN TO CAMELOT

A number of popular post–Cold War films (*Blue Sky* [1991], *Matinee* [1993], *The Nostradamus Kid* [1995], *Mulholland Falls* [1996], *The Butcher Boy* [1998], *The Iron Giant* [1998], *Blast From the Past* [1999], *Fail Safe* [2001], and *K-19: The Widowmaker* [2002]) situate their narratives temporally in the not-too-distant past of a generation or two ago. These movies devote significant resources in recreating the historical period in which Cold War tensions were heightened (1961 Berlin blockade, 1962 Cuban Missile Crisis) and the technologies of nuclear weapons became increasingly controversial (Strontium 90 fallout from atmospheric tests, public shelters), as did their delivery systems (post-Sputnik satellites, ICBMs, nuclear submarine–launched missiles).

At first glance these films may appear to present a nostalgic yearning for times gone by, the Eisenhower Happy Days or JFK's Camelot. This post–Cold War cluster of historical movies contrasts with the earlier 1980s nostalgia wave of period films (e.g., *Back to the Future* [1985], set principally in the 1950s) that promote the recent past as a golden age of prosperity and simplicity and distinctive from the *Falling Down* (1995) type of angst and alienation contemporary postmodern life engenders.[32] Scrutiny of how nuclear issues are presented in recent cinema's recounting of the early 1960s provides an emblematic window on the often conscious narrative efforts to make problematic the era's retrospective construction as a stereotypically simple and unsophisticated sociopolitical environment.

Blue Sky, like the earlier *Desert Bloom* (1986), revealed repressed familial sexual tensions of the era while detailing the covert U.S. atomic tests conducted underground during a bilateral moratorium with the Soviet Union. The black-and-white live-TV remake *Fail Safe* maintains the original novel's early 1960s' political and military ambience; and unlike the contemporized update of *On the Beach* (2001), it effectively relegates the nuclear threat to an anachronistic past. *K-19: The Widowmaker* shifts the focus onto the Soviet command and control system of the era in its depiction of a stricken submarine, with its inherent design flaws, close to a nuclear meltdown off the U.S. East Coast (a theme similarly covered in the HBO production *Hostile Waters* [1996], which recounts a near-catastrophic Soviet submarine accident from 1986). Most transparent in its problematic rendition of the Cuban Missile Crisis is *Thirteen Days* (2001), which draws heavily from decades of declassified Cold War security documents from both superpowers as well as recorded White House conversations of the time. Among the film's dramatic revelations are the failure of Kennedy's military and intelligence advisers to comprehend that the Soviets had given their troops in Cuba the discretion to use tactical nuclear weapons should U.S. forces invade the island and the fact that several Soviet IRBMs had operational warheads already in place.

In the Australian production *The Nostradamus Kid* the prospect of the world ending during the Cuban Missile Crisis provides its teen protagonist with a welcome pretext for seducing women. Similarly, *The Butcher Boy*'s strident anti-communism and dysfunctional Irish family milieu provides a backdrop of violent holocaust fantasies that counterpoint the mistrust and aggression constantly thrust upon an impressionable child. In *Mulholland Falls* a corrupt, quasi-fascist squad of Los Angeles police operating in the early 1960s become embroiled in a series of murders that implicates the U.S. military and the Atomic Energy Commission in a clandestine program of human radiation experiments. As such, the film is one of the few post–Cold War productions to overtly address the heinous nonconsensual experimentation that spanned the Cold War.[33]

The most inventive and refreshing of these historical dramas is the animated family feature *The Iron Giant.* Diametrically opposed to the Disney animation formula, which incessantly repeats archetypal plots and characters, this Warners Studio movie is set on the cusp of the 1960s in the seaside town of Rockwell, Maine. As in *Matinee,* the film draws intertextually from the fecund science fiction genre and official civil defense educational programs as it parodies post-Sputnik late night TV and high school atomic drills. When a boy finds and befriends a fallen alien robot, an unscrupulous national security investigator arrives and eventually brings about a nuclear strike on the town. The film marvelously allegorizes the nuclear arms race, the space race, and ufology but finds powerful narrative empathy in its plea for pacifism and restraint when confronting the unknown Other.

Of the films mentioned earlier, only *Blast From the Past* approximates a reactionary nostalgia. As a kooky Caltech nuclear scientist and his pregnant wife rush to their massive homemade backyard fallout shelter during the 1962 Cuba crisis, a stricken U.S. jet accidentally falls on their suburban Los Angeles home, which they immediately interpret as a direct nuclear strike on the city. The time-locked shelter doors are closed for thirty-five years because of an imagined "radiological half life" outside. Eventually, the scientist and his wife raise a boy (named Adam) from a huge library of liberal arts, language, and science texts alongside hokey conservative Mom and Popisms of the time. Entertainment comes in the form of looped 16 mm prints of *The Honeymooners* through a jerry-rigged rear projection TV or wholesome contemporary songs (e.g., Perry Como). For this neo-nuclear family time effectively stands still for three and a half decades.

As Adam passes age thirty-five he is sent into the world to bring back a mate, but only after his aging father has first ventured out for a quick reconnaissance trip fully dressed in a radiological protection suit and carrying a Geiger counter. What he encounters appalls him—bums raiding street trash, transsexual hookers soliciting, public vomiting, porn shops, and drive-by homeboys waving guns. This montage of millennium horrors is enough to send him scuttling back to the shelter, where he relates to his wife and son that the San Fernando Valley of their past has been reconstructed into a postholocaust nocturnal society of violent and depraved, sexually indeterminate mutants who feed off garbage and prowl the surface. But Adam's destiny and eagerness to explore surpass these disincentives, and he is soon experiencing the sun, sea, and sky of surface life. His comic encounters with late-twentieth-century Los Angeles, such as his first impressions of vehicular transportation, recall the common tropes of innocents abroad and fishes out of water. For Adam—a walking compendium of middle-American virtue and his parents' generational mores—the once virtual and phantasmic world of texts, photos, and oral history is made flesh; and he relishes his frequently incongruous, intellectual, and phenomenological interactions with it.

Much of the film's narrative concentrates on God-fearing Adam's idealized pursuit of knowledge and experience, as well as on the transformative power his near-messianic presence has on contemporary acquaintances.[34] As expressed in a late 1990s family TV series, Adam leaves in his wake the previously cynical and disaffected Los Angelinos, as if "touched by an angel."

Unsurprisingly, Adam does find a mate (Eve), and together t
parents back "home" and in from the cold (war). Using the now hy
IT stock his father bought nearly forty years earlier, Adam and Eve
new Eden for the elderly shelter dwellers. The couple fast-tracks the buildin
a replica 1960s home, retrofitted with period decor and furnishings but situated on its own lush acreage with million-dollar views. It's their own private
protectorate of nostalgia uncontaminated by the decaying world at the
millennium's passage.

Ultimately, Adam breaks the news to his father that there was no nuclear
attack on Los Angeles in 1962 and that their thirty-five-year subterranean
stasis was unnecessary. Given the desired simulacra of their improved current
environs, father and son agree that what they now have was worth it. But ever
the Cold Warrior, Adam's physicist father suspects the news of the Cold War
being over is merely expediency from the former Soviet Union, shrewdly
proposing "I bet the commies asked for aid," with which Adam concurs.

Hence, the film ends with a conventional conservative repatriation of traditional American values: monogamy, family, home, and capital where patriotism and patriarchy prevail. What is more, the finale suggests more than a hint
of skepticism about the permanence of the fall of communism and the utopian
promise of the post–Cold War Pax Americana.[35]

Blast From the Past makes for an interesting comparison with another post–
Cold War nuclear comedy, *Matinee,* which locates its entire narrative around
the time of the Cuba crisis. Cineaste director Joe Dante crafts a beguiling tale
that is as much about cinema history as it is about atomic fears. Unlike *Blast
From the Past,* Dante's film transcends nostalgia for affectionate homage in its
representation of JFK-era America.

The opening sequence brilliantly encapsulates Cold War sentiment in a
mock monster movie promotion that does more to deftly précis and critique
the genre in its few minutes of elapsed screen time than do most of the scholarly
volumes to date on science fiction cinema and the culture of nuclearism. After
a blinding flash engulfs the screen and fades to reveal a towering mushroom
cloud, a rapid montage of staple black-and-white Atomic Energy Commission
test films renders the bomb's concussive and heat effects on average suburban
family homes. The editing rapidly segues to a film trailer that teases the audience with familiar bombastic promises of chills and thrills while an entrepre-
neurial producer appears, in silhouette, to pitch his new screen sensation. Part
Alfred Hitchcock and part Roger Corman—but chiefly William Castle—the
fictitious Svengali turns to address the viewers as a title rolls "Introducing the
Screen's No. 1 Shock Expert":

rrible. But more terrible still are the effects
g] Hello, I'm Lawrence Woolsey, and I want
ing that could happen; something that *does*
ion picture. [Over stock footage of swarming
miniature marvel of social cooperation and
. if a man and an ant were exposed to
he result would be terrible indeed. For the

woman after another shrieking hysterically while being menaced by a giant claw from the fiendish, mostly off-camera Mant. The perspective then changes to reveal two youths (Gene Loomis and his brother Dennis) in a 1960s theater intently following the action. Woolsey reappears on the screen and occupies the entire frame:

> I feel I should warn you . . . the story of *Mant* is based on scientific *facts*; on theories that have appeared in national magazines. Yes, these terrible events could happen—in your town, in your home. And they *will* happen in this theatre, in Atomo-vision, the new motion picture miracle that puts *you* in the action.

In this brief sequence *Matinee* cannily and economically establishes the pop culture milieu that informs much of late 1950s and early 1960s science fiction cinema. The film effortlessly conflates paradigmatic iconography of the nuclear film genre via *Mant!*'s cinematic fusion of *Them!* (1954) with *The Fly* (1958). But this is no cheap shot at pastiche or lame parody. *Matinee* skillfully interrogates the conventions of the genre it is sympathetically lampooning with great conviction, knowledge, and humor.

The film locates its action near Florida's Key West naval base. Soon, this amiable display of Hollywood's coming attraction hucksterism is overshadowed by a televised presidential address outlining tensions resulting from the Soviet Union stationing ballistic missiles in Cuba—weapons capable of reaching Washington, D.C., and only ninety miles from Key West, the film's central location. Kennedy's naval blockade and the imminence of nuclear war are more than a narrative backdrop in *Matinee* since they permeate the expressed mood and sentiments of the lead and support characters. Junior high "duck-and-cover" drills are conducted, media and Conelrad updates punctuate the narrative, and panic buying at the town supermarket and the theater manager's bomb shelter are displayed prominently. The heightened tension of impending atomic doom is shown, to be further exploited by producer Woolsey. He rejects public criticism that he is expediently playing on nuclear fears during the crisis and justifies the use of his frightening "Atomo-vision" process and "Rumble-rama" exhibition trickery, saying: "It takes a lot more to scare people nowadays. They've got bombs that can kill half a million. There are people who haven't slept in years."

Hence *Mant!*, the delightful stereotype film-within-a-film, acts as a metatext for *Matinee's* own retrospective historical analysis. It invests the allegorical agenda of the invented fearful creature feature with a narrative counterpoint that usurps and reveals the period's official attempts at reifying nuclear weapons technologies and their function as omnicidal deterrents. *Mant!*, with its recognizably cheesy B-grade credentials, provides *Matinee* with the aporia of a culturally inscribed myth that defies reduction or further deconstruction. Perhaps paradoxically, it portrays its textual political unconscious on the surface—one that evades didacticism and that is delivered with comic grace.

Whereas *Blast From the Past* concentrates on the social and cultural dystopia of contemporary urban America, with only the slightest of veiled references to problems plaguing the Kennedy era, *Matinee* effortlessly touches on these ruptures in a way that deliberately makes problematic their historical recounting.[36] During a mock air raid drill, as terrified juveniles line their school's hallways crouched on their knees, a dissenting girl's voice is heard. She is shown being dragged to the principal's office while loudly protesting to all around her the futility of such exercises. Later, the troubled teenager relates to an inquisitive peer (and would-be boyfriend), Gene, whose absent father has been sent to the blockade, "all they teach you is lies. You bury your head while they build more bombs." This rebel *with* a cause explicitly challenges the convention of consensus, railing at institutionalized denial and the unquestioned social compliance of the inuring military-industrial complex. She also deflates Key West's own mythic status as a "wonderful place to live." Gene is later shown gripped in a nuclear nightmare, one in which he imagines witnessing his neighborhood demolished in an atomic attack.[37]

The scene is returned to typologically at *Matinee's* conclusion, where in an act of P. T. Barnum–like showmanship Woolsey has a third projector superimpose another film on top of *Mant!* The effect, shown in full color, produces an illusion that the screen itself has been blasted and burned away by a nuclear detonation outside the theater (a smoldering mushroom cloud appears in the background). The overlay is convincing enough to send the audience scurrying out of the theater and into the lobby (avoiding casualties from a collapsing platform). Again, we find *Matinee* skillfully negotiating complex individual and cultural responses to nuclear anxiety by evoking both personal pathology and its cultural exorcism through the catharsis of vicarious entertainment and mass spectacle.[38]

CONCLUSION

Of the 500 or so post–Cold War features that reference nuclear themes, the majority are U.S. productions. This figure represents an increase over the previous corresponding period by around 25 percent. That nuclear imagery and narratives are continuing to proliferate in this way suggests that nuclear concerns informing the production of media entertainments remain resilient themes of interest for filmmakers and audiences alike.

Despite the apparent easing of superpower tensions during this time, the prevailing imagery and narrative tropes maintain an existing trajectory of atomic anxiety, only momentarily disrupted by clusters of films where nuclear technologies are employed for peaceful or socially ameliorative purposes. In general, popular cinema continues to depict Russia and other former Soviet republics as potential, if not actual, enemies. The intersection of post–Cold War capital (market forces in a globalized economy) and communism's political repression is frequently depicted as merely providing opportunities for unreconstructed hard-liners to embrace the profits of nuclear black marketeering in an effort to bring back the good old days.

How nuclear movies will eventually negotiate the complex emotional and dramatic fallout from the 9/11 attacks and the ongoing war against terror(ism) remains to be seen, but as Jerome Shapiro and others cultural critics suggest, the deeply inscribed Judeo-Christian narrative of apocalypse will no doubt be pressed into service to make sense of our (fictive or ideological) endings.[39]

NOTES

1. See Dana Calvo and Robert Welkos, "Hollywood Shakes off Fear of Terror Images," *Los Angeles Times,* May 20, 2002; Bill Keller, "Nuclear Nightmares," *Los Angeles Times,* May 26, 2002; Kenneth Turan, "A Fearful Sum Recalculated," *Los Angeles Times,* June 23, 2002; Reed Johnson, "The Bomb Is Back," *Los Angeles Times,* June 18, 2002.

2. Francis Fukuyama, *The End of History and the Last Man* (New York: Free Press, 1992). I define a nuclear movie as any feature-length film, telemovie, or miniseries that overtly depicts or refers to nuclear technology. As I have argued elsewhere, some productions allegorize or use metaphors to make reference to their nuclear themes. See Mick Broderick, *Nuclear Movies* (Jefferson, NC: McFarland, 1991), xviii–xix.

3. See, for example, the promotional web site for the feature *Core* (2002), http://www.thecoremovie.com.

4. On postholocaust film, see Mick Broderick, "Heroic Apocalypse: *Mad Max,* Mythology and the Millennium," in *Crisis Cinema: The Apocalyptic Idea in Postmodern Narrative Film,* ed. Christopher Sharrett (Washington, DC: Maisonneuve, 1995), 250–

272. *Terminator 3* continues the generic impulse to depict a catastrophic global nuclear war as inevitable and a fait accompli. Unlike the premise of the first two Terminator films, it rejects the possibility of human agency delaying, disrupting, or preventing the forecast apocalyptic war from occurring. The final minutes depict, from an omniscient god's-eye view, ICBM strikes across the planet when the Skynet artificial intelligence takes control of the U.S. nuclear deterrent.

5. *MacGuffin* is a term adopted by Alfred Hitchcock to describe a major, although fundamentally superficial and interchangeable, element of plot motivation. For details on the specific application of narrative MacGuffins in nuclear cinema, see Broderick, *Nuclear Movies,* 5 and note; Kim Newman, *Millennium Movies: End of the World Cinema* (London: Titan, 1999), 70–71; Jerome Shapiro, *Atomic Bomb Cinema: The Apocalyptic Imagination on Film* (London: Routledge, 2002), 60–62.

6. Over the past few years a number of Marvel comics such as *Spiderman* have been adapted for film, including *X-Men* (2000), *X2* (2003), *Daredevil* (2003), and *The Hulk* (2003). These adaptations display shifting perceptions of nuclear themes. The *X-Men* mutants seem to be random biological offspring; however, one elder, Magneto, uses electromagnetic radiation to artificially create his own mutants and attempts to generate an enormous electromagnetic pulse effect from New York's Liberty Island to transform/contaminate the city's elite. *Daredevil* is blinded by biological waste, but many reviewers have erroneously construed this to be toxic nuclear waste—a telling critical laziness befalling many genre reviewers, such as those of *Eight Legged Freaks* (2002). *The Hulk,* however, retains the comic's specific nuclear origins and depicts a range of atomic effects from nuclear nightmares, a secret desert laboratory's self-destruction, gamma radiation accidents, mutation, and a military nuclear strike.

7. On Reagan's apocalyptic rhetoric, see Jeff Smith, "Reagan, Star Wars, and American Culture," *Bulletin of the Atomic Scientists* (January-February 1987); Michael Rogin, *Ronald Reagan: The Movie—and Other Episodes in Political Demonology* (Berkeley: University of California Press, 1988); Mick Broderick, "Surviving Armageddon: Beyond the Imagination of Disaster," *Science Fiction Studies* 20, 3 (1993): 362–382.

8. The U.S. policy to see "regime change" in Iraq is entertained in *Deterrence* (2000), in which a future Jewish president of the United States annihilates the city of Baghdad with a 20 mega-ton thermonuclear weapon after Saddam Hussein again invades an Arab neighbor. With Hussein, like Osama bin Laden, missing and presumed dead, the U.S. Congress is challenging presidential "state of the union" claims that Iraq was in possession of, or attempting to procure, nuclear weapons technologies that presented a clear and present danger, warranting invasion. Meanwhile, North Korea, a bellicose nation with undisputed nuclear ambitions, publicly threatens its regional neighbors and the United States with nuclear recriminations should the country be preemptively attacked.

9. See Paul Brians, *Nuclear Holocausts: Atomic War in Fiction, 1895–1984* (Kent, OH: Kent State University Press, 1987); Paul Boyer, *When Time Shall Be No More: Prophetic Belief In Modern American Culture* (Cambridge: Harvard University Press,

1992); Frank Kermode, "Waiting for the End," in *Apocalypse Theory and the Ends of the World,* ed. Malcolm Bull (Oxford: Blackwell, 1995), 250–263; Mick Broderick, "Apocalyptic Desire," *Peace Journal* 8: 2 (1996): 267–271; Shapiro, *Atomic Bomb Cinema.*

10. See Owen Greene, Ian Percival, and Irene Ridge, *Nuclear Winter: The Evidence and the Risks* (New York: B. Blackwell, 1985), and National Research Council, *The Effects on the Atmosphere of a Major Nuclear War* (1985).

11. "Nuclear Notebook: Russian Nuclear Forces," *Bulletin of the Atomic Scientists* (July–August 2002): 71–73; "Nuclear Notebook: U.S. Nuclear Forces," *Bulletin of the Atomic Scientists* (May–June 2002): 70–75.

12. My thanks to Jonathan Parfrey, executive director, Physicians for Social Responsibility (Los Angeles), for pointing this out.

13. See Bruce Blair, "Nuclear Y2K Dangers in Russia," Brookings Institute, http://www.brookings.org (1999); Blair, "Weapons and Y2K," *NewsHour With Jim Lehrer,* PBS, December 30, 1999.

14. The closest such event was the failure of a spy satellite. As Steven Lee Meyers reported in the *New York Times* on January 2, 2000: "A computer failure caused by the arrival of the year 2000 cut communications with one of the nation's secret spy satellites for two to three hours on Friday night and continued to hobble its operations today, Pentagon officials said. A computer system at a ground station of the National Reconnaissance Office, the agency that runs the military's spy satellites, failed at 7 P.M. Eastern time on Friday, or midnight Greenwich Mean Time, the standard to which many military systems are synchronized." http://www.fas.org/sgp/news/2000/01/nyt010200.html.

15. This is in keeping with 1950s Cold War science fiction films such as *The Beast From 20,000 Fathoms* (1953) and *Killers From Space* (1954), where nuclear technologies do destroy the alien or monstrous threat.

16. This imagery of a massive craft poised above a city, repeated and fetishized interminably throughout the film, provides a metaphor of the nuclear age. Once intercontinental delivery systems were established, any city on the globe could be destroyed virtually without warning. The Damoclean sword and living beneath the "shadow of the bomb" provide a perfect referent for the ominous alien spacecraft featured in *ID4*.

17. See Fredric Jameson, *Postmodernism, or, the Cultural Logic of Late Capitalism* (Duham, NC: Duke University Press, 1991). *ID4* makes for an interesting comparison with *Mars Attacks!* (1997), released two years later. Tim Burton's film also has an impatient military intelligence clique desperate to persuade the president to use atomic weapons to "nuke the bastards," but it is only at the brink of world collapse that the commander-in-chief relents. What transpires is among the most surreal scenes in recent mainstream cinema. The ICBM rushes toward the Martian craft, only to be intercepted by a bizarre-looking device that combines a mouthpiece, horn, and balloon. At the point of nuclear impact/detonation the Martian instrument rapidly expands and absorbs the massive blast. Perfunctorily, the device returns to the Martian ship where the lead alien *inhales* all the contents from the

instrument, makes a rude blurting noise, and cackles defiantly. Incredulous, the despondent U.S. joint chief shrugs, "What the hell *was* that?!" The nuclear deterrent is totally ineffective. Liberation must come from elsewhere.

18. For a more extensive exploration of such themes in *ID4*, see Michael Rogin's brilliant short monograph *Independence Day, or How I Learned to Stop Worrying and Love the Enola Gay* (London: British Film Institute, 1998).

19. Nuclear submarine tales continued into the post–Cold War era with box office hits *The Hunt for Red October* (1991) and *Crimson Tide* (1995). In both instances prevailing Cold War sentiments remain through continued nuclear brinkmanship. More recently, *K-19: The Widowmaker* (2002) implicates the arms race as inherently unsafe even to the point of compromised and faulty technologies, where early unstable Soviet submarines are nicknamed the "Hiroshima" class.

20. In late July 2002 a 2-kilometer-wide asteroid (2002 NT7) was reportedly on a collision course with earth, with an anticipated arrival date of early 2019. Later estimates now downplay the likelihood of such an event, although 2060 has not been ruled out. See Don Yoemans, "Asteroid 2002 NT7: Potential Earth Impact in 2019 Ruled Out," http://neo.jpl.nasa.gov/news/news133.html, dated July 28, 2002.

21. Potential celestial collisions also inspired other nuclear productions, including the post–Cold War telemovie *Asteroid* (1996) and its Cold War disaster predecessors *When Worlds Collide* (1951), *Meteor* (1979), and *Night of the Comet* (1984).

22. Marginalized, working-class heroes die in the act of delivering their nuclear payloads in all three films—an alcoholic, former Vietnam pilot, and alien abductee (Randy Quaid) in *ID4*; a washed-up and forgotten Apollo astronaut (Robert Duvall) in *Deep Impact*; and a single-parent "grease monkey" (Bruce Willis) in *Armageddon*. The trope is also repeated in *Space Cowboys* (2000), in which a group of NASA washouts are unwittingly sent into orbit to capture a former Soviet nuclear weapons platform that both Russia and the United States deny exists.

23. Even *A Beautiful Mind* (2001) plays with nuclear terrorism, employing a key subplot suggesting that a brilliant mathematician is part of a covert operation to uncover an enemy plot to assemble an atomic device for detonation in America. The clandestine project is revealed, however, to be no more than the scholar's ongoing schizophrenic hallucinations, although in keeping with the then national security paranoia of the Cold War.

24. Tony Bennett and Janet Woollacott, *Bond and Beyond* (London: Routledge, 1986), 18.

25. Even the Bond film distributor's publicity makes the point, calling the " 'classic' Bond films (as nos. 1–16 are now referred to) [a] memory, a past associated with the pre-Glasnost era." See James Chapman, *License to Thrill: A Cultural History of the James Bond Films* (New York: Columbia University Press, 1999), 252.

26. *Austin Powers*'s nuclear plot also closely resembles that of *Octopussy* (1983). Of the twenty Bond films released prior to 2002, only five avoid overt reference or significant plot elements involving nuclear technologies; see Broderick, *Nuclear Movies*, 30–33.

27. Brosnan also starred as a secret agent in the post–Cold War nuclear telemovie *Alastair Mclean's Death Train* (1997), saving the world from a renegade Russian general's bid to launch a superpower war.

28. A gala premiere was meant to celebrate the French navy's official cooperation in the film but was cancelled following a *Le Monde* interview with the star who applauded the Pacific protests of Greenpeace and said, "I will never be convinced that nuclear arms are good for peace." Quoted in *Sydney Morning Herald,* December 4, 1995.

29. At the time of release, the characterization by Denise Richards was ridiculed, since she appears in microshorts and singlet while portraying a "noo-cu-lar" scientist charged with overseeing the dismantling and destruction of Russian warheads. However, this casting and costuming are not so inconsistent with the tradition of other Bond "girls" and femmes fatales or no more preposterous than the mythology and iconography of Bond himself. Indeed, the same reservations were expressed about Nicole Kidman in *The Peacemaker*. These issues were amusingly alluded to in the romantic comedy *Notting Hill* (2000), when Julia Roberts, self-consciously playing Hollywood's actress du jour, is shown studying dialogue for a forthcoming thriller in which she has to master and prattle off complicated text concerning nuclear technologies.

30. In *Diplomatic Siege* (2000) Serbian terrorists are similarly responsible for a nuclear crisis at a captured U.S. Embassy in Romania, where a secret A-bomb is set to explode.

31. One remarkably optimistic calculation occurs when Ryan tries to convince a Pentagon general of the importance of his information and his need to access the hotline. He suggests that 20–25 million American lives depend on it. This would appear a serious underestimate, given the anticipated Russian first strike would not be limited to a counterforce salvo.

32. See Andrew Britten, "Blissing Out: The Politics of Reaganite Entertainment," *The Movie* 31–32 (1984): 1–42; Vivian Sobchack, "Postfuturism," in *Screening Space: The American Science Fiction Film* (New York: Ungar, 1987), 223–305.

33. During the early 1990s the Clinton administration conducted an extensive inquiry into these human guinea pig tests, which involved thousands of Americans. The resulting report of the Presidential Committee into Human Radiation Experiments can be found at http://tis.eh.doe.gov/ohre/. Other films that overtly depict such experiments include *Fat Man and Little Boy* (1989, aka *The Shadow Makers*), which describes Manhattan Project scientists involved in secret plutonium injections, and *Spontaneous Combustion* (1990) in which a pregnant woman is deliberately exposed to a nuclear test. Such experiments did occasionally make it into Cold War film, however, although usually expressed in terms of allegory and metaphor via the horror and science fiction genres. See Mick Broderick, "Nuclear *Frisson*: Cold War Cinema and Human Radiation Experiments," *Film/Literature Quarterly* 27, 3 (1999): 196–201. In *The Hulk,* what at first appears to be a child's nuclear nightmare, related as "screen memory" in reaction to childhood trauma, is revealed to be an actual

event—witnessing the atomic detonation of a secret weapons laboratory in the U.S. desert.

34. When Adam first appears from underground, a washed-up and destitute shop owner mistakes him for "the Son" and later gathers fellow New Agers to worship at a makeshift shrine near the fallout shelter's elevator entrance.

35. Significantly, the song that plays over the end credits is a Randy Newman song that cheerfully expresses a popular American sentiment about nuking the planet, friend and foe alike, because "nobody likes us, so let's drop the big one now . . . let's drop the big one now."

36. One rare moment for potential critical reflection comes within moments of Adam first walking the LA streets when he excitedly approaches an African American postal worker and shakes her hand, delighted at last to meet "a Negro!"

37. Unlike Gene, *The Butcher Boy*'s sociopathic child antihero relishes the thanatological fantasy of walking among the nuclear dead of his oppressive village.

38. See Mick Broderick, "Witnessing the Unthinkable: A Meditation on Film and Nuclear Sublime," *Antithesis* (Spring 1992): 67–75.

39. See Shapiro, *Atomic Bomb Cinema,* 62–72.

American Monument
The Waste Isolation Pilot Plant

Peter C. van Wyck

March 26, 1999. Carlsbad, N.M.—Energy Secretary Bill Richardson today announced that the first shipment of defense-generated transuranic radioactive waste arrived safely at the U.S. Department of Energy's (DOE) Waste Isolation Pilot Plant (WIPP). Hundreds of people were on hand to watch this important milestone in the Energy Department's work to permanently dispose of defense-generated transuranic waste left from the research and production of nuclear weapons. . . . "This is truly a historic moment—for the Department of Energy and the nation," said Secretary Richardson. "This shipment to WIPP represents the beginning of fulfilling the long-overdue promise to all Americans to safely clean up the nation's Cold War legacy of nuclear waste and protect the generations to come."

—U.S. Department of Energy, press release, March 26, 1999

The place is Carlsbad, New Mexico.[1] A very large hole has been excavated deep within the hard indifference of the desert's sedimentary salt. It is the world's first permanent underground storage facility for nuclear waste—stunningly expensive and equally controversial. In 1999 the Department of Energy, under the auspices of the U.S. government, approved the transport of transuranic (and thus very persistent) nuclear waste into this hole.

Sometime around 2035 the hole will be filled to capacity and sealed shut. And then an extraordinary series of events will begin to unfold. By decree of the government, a very large monument—in keeping with the magnitude of the burial beneath—must be constructed to mark the site. It will be perhaps the largest public works project in modern history. But this marker, this gravestone monument, must serve both more and less than a commemorative purpose. Indeed, this monument must seek to *not* commemorate, for what lies beneath must never be celebrated yet in some fashion must always be remembered. It therefore cannot be a typical monument. It cannot be allowed to content itself as a monument to the present; it is not something we wish to remember, nor is it something for which we wish to be remembered. It must, again by decree, convey a very specific message to the future, and the message it must convey is: Go Away! This monument to waste must perform the threat that lies beneath. And it must do so for a legislated period of 10,000 years—until approximately the year 12035. An ordinal number that should not be allowed to conceal its deeply cardinal implications: 300 generations, a Y12K problem.

It is a singular meeting of the material and the semiotic. And it is an enormous wager that hinges on making waste safe—through burial—then making it dangerous again—through signification. In it must persist the groundless hope that the semiotic decomposition of the sign takes place at a slower rate than the nuclear decomposition of the waste itself.

NOT YET

Imagine the perplexity of a man outside time and space who has lost his watch, and his measuring rod, and his tuning fork. I believe, Sir, that it is indeed this state which constitutes death.

—Alfred Jarry

It's all happening at the edges. At the edge of the social, at the edge of the imagination, at the edge of memory and the edge of the probable. No bodies, nobody; there is no one there. Except, that is, in the drawings of the design ideas. There are quite a number of them. Tiny humans at the cemetery for waste.

True, it is a convention of sorts to do this—in certain kinds of documentary photography, that is. Sometimes one sees a scale of some kind, a measuring stick propped up along the cleanly excavated face of an archaeological dig—there to show the size of the object pictured. And sometimes it's just an appendage or a miscellaneous article of use. In any case, the intention is to communicate the size of an object and in doing so to inject into it a comparative and documentary veracity. This is what allows this kind of image to show—it is a measuring rod by other means.

8.1 Spike Field. This is an image of a design for the desert monument. Concept by Michael Brill; art by Safdar Abidi. This image and others reproduced in this chapter are free of copyright and are taken from Kathleen M. Trauth, Stephen C. Hora, and Robert V. Guzowski, Expert Judgment on Markers to Deter Inadvertent Human Intrusion Into the Waste Isolation Pilot Plant *(Albuquerque: Sandia National Laboratories, 1983).*

But here, in these images, here we see little humans, as if not only to ground the magnitude of the monuments but to give them a place in the world. The humans are not there to show the size of a pottery shard or the length of a femur but to illustrate the fact that these images are to be understood as part of a world—our world.

In addition to the measuring rod, there is also a watch and a tuning fork—pieces of technology that mark time and the epoch of the discovery rather than size. Without them these photographs would seem to be fantastic drawings culled from an archive of Roger Dean's album artwork. So they are there, these humans, there where they are not supposed to be.

To take the human away would be to present the unthinkable possibility that no one might be around to see it. It is "psychologically" necessary to show how a human might relate to the monstrous fact of these installations. The images need the uncanny to make them intelligible. The human must be there as the index of the inhuman, as the zero degree of the strange. A home, or at least an *oikos,* is required such that the strange may find its place elsewhere. The strangeness of the monuments requires a home to convey their very strangeness.

And they sure are big; to this the little humans attest—so much so that the little humans are perhaps the only choice for a scale. What else would work? These people are so fragile and so small somehow. There is monumental duration on the one side, finite mortality on the other. The monument stands for a geological permanence and the human for its dutiful respondent. How can one possibly guarantee the other? In one sense they must. For it is the task of the monuments to keep humans away and the task of the humans to keep away.

You don't have to look far to discover a problem. One *sees* the problem: what *are* they doing there? The problem operates in an immediate and visual register. How else? These monuments are haunted by their own failure, even in advance of their construction. As *ideas,* they carry the humans into the region from which they are to be excluded; that is, humans are parasitically present within the very gesture that would seek to guarantee their absence. As with other forms of contemporary wilderness, the human is always present, one way or another.

But even in this there is a strange and visceral sense of having one's body there. For me it is the little human that stands before the Menacing Earthworks. I would like to be there—there to witness the place in the desert where this will take place. And it will *take* the place—take it out of a series of "present" moments into a distinct series of futures. Not history as the site of the now but the present as the site of the "not yet." This is the particular messianism of threat. Not yet.

This is not to say the threat is somehow distant, pointing to a future only as if it weren't both immediate and present. It is. The point is that the threat—as threat—has the status of a paradoxical event. On one hand it is something that is in advance of the accident, something in advance of that which befalls. But on the other hand, to be under threat is for something to have already taken place. To be under the threat of nuclear contamination is for *many* things to have already taken place.[2]

The rise of contemporary technological innovations brings with it correspondingly more complex accident scenarios. But the differences consist in more than mere complexity (if complexity can be mere). From the point of view of large social-political assemblages, a more complex (but arbitrary) series is required (e.g., capital, labor, land, unemployment, poverty, trailer parks, hurricane casualties). It is no longer possible to think of practice and accident as temporally and functionally distinct. The practice contains the accident, not simply as a possibility—as that which may or may not happen—but fully and completely as virtuality.

DREAD

I wonder what the body would feel like as it stands in the desert in the presence of such a monument, knowing it to be a place like no other. How can one respond to the singularity of the place, to the negative intention of the monument (except by being there)? The figure in the drawing is doing what most would do. It stands in a pose that recalls contemplation. What else? This is an entirely conventional expectation of what monuments do—they inspire contemplation and perhaps awe. But contemplative is the right word only if we keep in mind its nonmystical connotation. It is a bringing together of a sense of viewing or witnessing strictly with that of a *templum*—a site marked out for observation of the auguries. Together it is a site and a practice, a site of memory and a site of awe.

But in this case the issue *is* the memory. Which is to say, a forgetfulness. I cannot remember, and even if I can, it is a memory that is singular and particular, not social, deliberate, or collective. Contemplation must run aground in the site of memory where the memory itself is absent. In this sense the contemplative posture of the human witnesses is precisely wrong. The contemplative posture finds its home in a commemoration. What must be recalled here, what must be rendered sensible by the monument, is an utterly singular past. And regardless of whatever else one might like to attribute to it, it is a past that must be understood as dangerous (literally) to the present. It is a past that persists into the present, that impinges on us in a way that makes concrete that which was symbolic or virtuous: the dependence of the present upon the respectful understanding of the past. Not a past that is "significant" to the present or a past that is "worthy" of recollection insofar as it is understood to be the laboratory of the present. Rather, a past that actually persists in the form of a threat to the present.

What is concealed in the image, like the waste that lies concealed beneath, is dread. Kierkegaard's dread—as an anxiety with respect to the future—is present here in the realization that the past persists only in the possibility of its repetition, that is, in the future.[3] It is because the past has not been allowed to *be past* that dread or anxiety is produced (for if the past were really past, one could not feel dread but only repentance, says Kierkegaard). The very possibility that the past invoked by the monument can persist and repeat into the future is what realizes dread—dread of and for the future as the past's repetition.

SECRET

This desert I am interested in will be a place that will house an enormous secret, a secret that must be kept and always disclosed—simultaneously.

In a way this is a sure bet. That is, there is a sense in which this requirement for secrecy and disclosure will most certainly be met, for several reasons. The first concerns the fact that this is a project about limits. Everything about the WIPP and the monument operates in a complex relation to a limit. At the limit of civilization—its place is the desert, the other American wilderness. At the limit of history—its time is the deep future. At the limit of meaning—its witness is unknown, abstract, and indeterminate. At the limit of the symbolic—auguring the language of the future is a dizzying confrontation with the aporias that obtain when one steps outside of the frame of the present. At the limit of technology—the ability to engineer materials for this unprecedented duration is and remains hypothetical at best. Distributed throughout these limit regions, failure and certainty are asymptotically related (and the wager is that the oracular abilities of technoscientific expertise may correctly divine the intersection of the two series).

Yet these things constitute only one dimension of the layers of concealment involved. The other dimension (or perhaps "another dimension"; there may be more than one) has to do with what we might call the epistemological anchoring of the monument. The anchoring of meanings—produced through reversal and inversion, whereby certain fundamental discursive concepts are covertly recast in light of the burial endeavor—is secret as well. Here responsibility is shifted from its ideological affinity for the "individual"—particularly the living individual—and his or her autonomy toward a future that must be alerted to the presence of the interred waste. In the same way, justice must proceed not from the rights of the living individual but from the distributive rights of future persons—that is, persons not yet living. And national safety (together with its institutional spokesperson, risk analysis) shifts from the Cold War strategy of being as dangerous as possible to remain safe to its opposite: becoming as safe as possible to preserve the possibility of being dangerous. It is far more complicated than this, but I wish to convey here only the general structure of secrecy: both inside and outside of discourse, both inside and outside of the monument, the project in the desert is prefaced by and organized under a structural secret.

The second sense in which the requirement for secrecy and disclosure will be met, which in a way preempts the first, is that secrets are just like that; that is, they tend to secrete. Occasional theorists of the secret, Gilles Deleuze and Félix Guattari, have put it this way:

> The secret has a privileged, but quite variable relation to perception
> and the imperceptible. The secret relates first of all to certain contents.
> The content is *too* big for its form . . . or else the contents themselves

have a form, but that form is covered, doubled, or replaced by a simple container, envelope, or box whose role is to suppress formal relations.[4]

And furthermore:

[T]hese are contents it has been judged fitting to isolate or disguise for various reasons. Drawing up a list of these reasons (shame, treasure, divinity, etc.) has limited value as long as the secret is opposed to its discovery as in a binary machine having only two terms, the secret and disclosure, the secret and desecration.[5]

Thus, it is only as an anecdotal formulation that the disclosure of the secret is its opposite. From the point of view of the concept, however, the perception of the secret is part of it. To paraphrase Deleuze and Guattari, the secret must move through society as a fish through water but on the condition that society behave toward the secret as water to fish. The secret is a social function, a social assemblage.

This is the institutional figure of the secret in the desert: a material with contents too big for its form. It is a container of secrets that exceeds itself. It is in this sense that the "significant" part of nuclear material is its own remainder. The U.S. strategy has been to manage the material (not the remainder) through concealment and selective disclosure. From the point of view of the U.S. government, one could say there are two secrets rather than one: on the one hand the burial and on the other the sign. The burial of the waste operates as the justification for the design and placement of the marker. And the marker operates as the ethical alibi for the interment of the waste. Both conceal a secret operation, and each operates as the standard-bearer for the other. The marker will operate through the deployment of enduring signs of danger to signify the danger below.

Yet the precise nature of the danger is incidental to the intention of the sign. The signification of this sign—which from this point of view would be the relation between the form and substance of a contents (the waste and its emanations) and the form and substance of expression (the monument as a system of communication and containment)—must exceed the simple idiom of the monument in every imaginable way. The important thing is that there is no way to reduce the monument to a straightforward relationship between a signifier and a signified, or recto-verso, where materiality is on one side only. The secret operates the way it does because the sign is already doubled—there is substance and form on *both* sides. Nonetheless, the sign's real function is to efface the burial—this is the other secret of the sign. The sign's double mission is to efface the waste and to remain "dangerous." And the burial, ostensibly the thing that supports the sign, is allowed to remain secret.

Peter C. van Wyck

The secreted (radioactive) materials, part of the contents in this case, have a very slippery relationship to their form. In a sense, the materials themselves are not dangerous; rather, it's what is expelled that presents a hazard. On the one hand, without the particularity of the contents as substance, the material could not have the actual form it has, but on the other hand, the form of the contents is only probabilistic (i.e., the decay series of half-lives), related back to the state of the contents at a given moment, an arrangement that can only be known through some kind of disclosure or leak: "[T]he secret has a way of spreading that is in turn shrouded in secrecy. The secret as secretion. The secret must sneak, insert, or introduce itself into the arena of public forms: it must pressure them and prod known subjects into action."[6] Thus secrets can never be perfectly secretive, can never win the struggle against disclosure, for they are not in opposition to it.

Consider the example of the Stealth aircraft mentioned by Jean Baudrillard.[7] A Stealth aircraft is paradigmatically a contents that presents no form (it is the precise opposite of a decoy); that is what allows it to remain unseen. Indeed, as Baudrillard points out, early versions of these aircraft were so transparent, so invisible, that they were unable to locate even themselves (resulting in several rather expensive crashes). These prototypes were too secretive. There has to be some relationship to perception, to the perceptible—"something must ooze from the box," say Deleuze and Guattari. Or, from Baudrillard's perspective, "as is well-known, when playing hide-and-seek, you should never make your-self too invisible, or the others will forget about you."[8] And this, he surmises, is the reason the Stealth aircraft—even though it was a "high-level" secret—was presented to the public to begin with.[9]

Clearly, the secret exists in relation to the visible and not just to perception per se. The danger of the waste, although not visible, is not even on the order of the visible as such. (And this, I would add, is critical to all thought about eco-logical and nuclear threats.) Yet the materials to be interred, the materials that present the danger, are precisely on the order of the visible, and this is why they have chosen to conceal them beneath the desert. Thus, there are two sorts of relations to secrecy: one on the order of an invisible visible—the concealed, the buried, the stealth, hide and seek; and the other on the order of an absolute invisibility—radioactive emanations and ecological threats generally.[10] In the latter case, nuclear toxicity operates necessarily outside the register of sight. It requires mediation to be disclosed, a relay into a signifying semiotic regime: a Geiger counter to render it sonorous or a body or tissue that the invisible alpha and beta particles and gamma radiation transform. In other words, nothing renders its toxicity visible; it can only relay into the order of the visible via the

156

production of signs (signals, sounds, symptoms). In the former sense, that of an invisible visible, the transuranic material, the dross—whether beneath the ground or heaped on the surface—always contains within it another sort of secret (the significant part of its story left untold). It is a secret of a different order and one disclosed by very different means.

In the initial planning phases of the Waste Isolation Pilot Plant project in the early 1980s, the option of not marking the waste at all was seriously considered—the idea being that if it were really well hidden and hidden in a place where no one would ever think of looking for it or anything else, the safety of the present and the future would be secured.[11] By 1985, however, the possibility that a disposal site could be designed without a permanent marker system was specifically excluded by the Environmental Protection Agency ("Disposal sites shall be designated by the most permanent markers"[12]). If, in other words, the wastes were hidden too well, one might simply forget that they were there and discover either them or their secretions by "accident."

FIGURE

This panel member therefore recommends that the markers and the structures associated with them be conceived along truly gargantuan lines. To put their size into perspective, a simple berm, say 35 meters wide and 15 meters high, surrounding the proposed land-withdrawal boundary, would involve the excavation, transport, and placement of around 12 million m^3 of earth. What is proposed of course, is on a much grander scale than that. By contrast, in the construction of the Panama Canal, 72.6 million m^3 were excavated and the Great Pyramid occupies 2.4 m^3. In short, to ensure probability of success, the WIPP marker undertaking will have to be one of the greatest public works ventures in history.

—Frederick Newmeyer[13]

The secretions I have pointed to are not only a structural necessity of the secret per se but also exist in a relation to obligation. The obligation in this case has played out in a number of ways but perhaps most profoundly in the manner in which the problem of marking waste has been addressed.

In 1983 several scholars were asked to prepare reports on aspects of waste burial and marking systems; these reports established the organizing themes that were to direct and shape subsequent deliberations on the questions of both storage and marking schemes. The group, known as the Human Interference Task Force, worked under this set of assumptions: there is an ethical responsibility to reduce risk for future persons; the obligation to the future can be discharged if sufficient knowledge is made available to them; future persons are assumed to be capable of breaching any repository design; and they would be presumed to have some basic knowledge of physics.[14]

Should future persons elect to breach the repository, they and not the present generation would be responsible. Therefore, the marker's ethical function works in two directions. It will allow those who should know better to avert the danger. And for those who either cannot figure it out or do not care, the present cannot be held ethically negligent. In either case the obligation of the present has been met.

Some of the works carried out on behalf of the DOE were indeed remarkable. The most astonishing contribution to the development of the marker was authored by Thomas Sebeok. His work (the only significant contribution from the American semiotic world) was in part a semiotic primer and introduced some concepts of information theory as well—it particularly reinforced the idea of "redundancy" as the key hedge against temporal semiotic decomposition. But for Sebeok the problem was bigger than this. First and foremost he viewed it as a question of the sign's stability through time. His first recommendation was:

> that information be launched and artificially passed on into the short-term and long-term future with the supplementary aid of folkloristic devices, in particular a combination of an artificially created and nurtured ritual-and-legend. The most positive aspect of such a procedure is that it need not be geographically localized, or tied to any one language-and-culture.[15]

The idea was that the present would design a kind of epistemological false trail such that people would be disinclined even to visit the site. And this disinclination would not necessitate any knowledge of the meaning of the site or of the nature of the materials interred. "A ritual annually renewed can be foreseen, with the legend retold year-by-year (with, presumably, slight variations)."[16]

However, the hacking of a contemporary mythological deep structure, the manufacture of a new tradition designed to secure the site, was in Sebeok's view insufficient. In addition, he saw the need for a transhistorical assembly of experts. The "truth" of the site

> would be entrusted to—what we might call for dramatic emphasis—an "atomic priesthood," that is, a commission of knowledgeable physicists, experts in radiation sickness, anthropologists, linguists, psychologists, semioticians, and whatever additional expertise may be called for now, and in the future. Membership in the "priesthood" would be self-selective over time.[17]

Thus defined, the nuclear Templars would be charged with mythological supervision and the production of metamessages as necessary. Should future generations fail to obey the imperative to care for the site,

> the atomic priesthood would be charged with the added responsibility
> of seeing to it that our behest, as embodied in the cumulative sequence
> of metamessages, is to be heeded—if not for legal reasons, then for
> moral reasons, with *perhaps the veiled threat* that to ignore the mandate
> would be tantamount to inviting some sort of supernatural retribution.[18]

As profoundly cynical as Sebeok's proposal may appear, he nonetheless saw very clearly the futility of merely launching a sign into the future. The pragmatics of the sign—the work it must do—at least makes Sebeok's proposal a plausible thought experiment.

A second area of research was concerned less with the sign itself than with cultural supports maintaining knowledge of nuclear waste sites and their locations. A. Weitzberg wrote a paper entitled *Building on Existing Institutions to Perpetuate Knowledge of Waste Repositories.*[19] The paper focused on techniques for deploying existing systems of "information" archives (libraries, online databases, national archives, maps, geodetic surveys). The deployment of existing practices of knowledge, from maps to periodic tables, has since become an important feature of marker design proposals. There are two things of note here: the first is the idea of an archive as a place where knowledge can survive independent of a culture that produced it; the second is the implicit assumption that information (i.e., data) is equivalent to knowledge to begin with. Nonetheless, this paper addressed an important, if obvious, concern that the marker itself could not be solely counted on as the source of information about waste.

From the concern for the sign and the question of the archive, we come to a third area of research: the human. The work of Percy Tannenbaum focused on what he saw as universal characteristics of the human perceptual makeup.[20] Determining these basic elements of human perception—whether facial expression or fear reactions to menacing figures—became a prominent theme in discussions concerning the philosophy of the marker design. Made up of equal parts of Jungian and behaviorist theory, a design that could be propped up by an essential human dimension became a seductive proposition—in other words, the question of whether a sign could iconically point to human fear.[21] This line of inquiry is fascinating, as it tends to outflank the semiotic and archival questions by appealing to human perception at a deep structure level.

The last area of research I will mention amounts to a kind of pragmatic, historically based semiotics. The archaeologist Maureen Kaplan did some significant work in this area by framing the problem of the marker as a historical one.[22]

To address this, she suggested a four-level taxonomy for how information should be conveyed, from the very simple to the very complex—something is here; it is dangerous; it is dangerous, and here is why you should go away; and finally, here is some detailed symbolic information. This taxonomy was based not only on a need for redundancy but on an assumption that interpretive strategies, languages, and symbolic competencies change and will continue to do so.

Kaplan created a pragmatic taxonomy of layered messages by making use of the theoretical support derived from Sebeok's flagging of redundancy and working with the idea that there are culturally neutral, transhistorical signs that would invoke human fear. Although this new taxonomy informed almost all subsequent design ideas, it is important to see that at this point in the development of the marker project the problem was granted considerable complexity. As government-funded research, this was the case less and less frequently.

Building on the work of the Human Interference Task Force, two new teams were recruited in 1990: the Markers Panel.[23] Numerous disciplines were represented: materials science, architecture, environmental design, anthropology, linguistics, archaeology, astronomy, communications, geomorphology, scientific illustration, semiotics, and environmental engineering. Perhaps not surprisingly, both teams approached the problem as a kind of time-capsule puzzle. They were to a certain extent interested in the materials that would be utilized, their foreseeable durability, and so on; but their principle concern was how to design a system of marking that would convey the danger of the site.

It was clear to the teams that to rely on language, on written texts, to carry the burden of meaning was dangerous. But both teams also felt textual accounts of the area were necessary, at least for the near future (100–500 years). The presumption of linguistic mutation and perhaps even the emergence of unique languages over such a period set up a kind of internal tension with respect to the polysemiosis. Both teams more or less followed the leveled message taxonomy mentioned earlier, and both acknowledged the idea that linguistic indeterminacy did not foreclose the use of signs. However, apart from the informational aspects of the design, both teams approached the problem of the marker as though the site itself could be made to *look* dangerous. The design would not in fact be dangerous; it would signify danger.

FUTURE

All of this has been directed toward the future. The desert monument as archive is a passive sender of information directed at future persons on a need-to-know

8.2 Landscape of thorns. Concept by Michael Brill; art by Safdar Abidi.

basis. In this sense the monument disavows the present, disavows that the material is dangerous now in the present, and disavows that it has been dangerous since it came into being. And significantly, it disavows the assertion of its own presence as a massive production in the desert.[24] This set of disavowals allows the monument to be placed, as it were, facing away from us, facing always toward the future, as though it were not intended to recall any past in particular. The future witness to the monument is called upon to understand only the site itself, not the reason the waste is there, not the reason the waste came to be waste, and certainly not any sense of how we as de facto authors and custodians of this waste might feel about having been responsible in various measure for producing it. Nothing, in other words, that might convey the basic truth that, were we to reflect on it, we could only feel a profound shame and sorrow with respect to a toxified future.

What remains at a distance in all of this is that the disaster is not in the future; it has already happened (and, to paraphrase Cathy Caruth,[25] we have survived without knowing it). The monument can only feign its prophylaxis, feign the impartiality of description when perhaps something more in the shape of a confession is called for.[26]

MONUMENT

So what is being asked here? If we consider the desert problem as one of simply making a monument endure, we have perhaps unwittingly produced a problem of a merely technical nature—a problem solvable (one would suppose) with better design and more enduring materials. On the other hand, if we consider the problem to be one of making a monument not only endure but "mean" for the prescribed period, we have an utterly different sort of problem. In fact, we have not one but two problems side by side.

Let us say that if the first problem concerns meaning and its projection into the future, then the second must concern the vehicle of this transmission—that is, the monument itself. And once put this way, one might begin to ask certain questions concerning meaning and monuments. For instance, is the monument proposed for the nuclear waste burial even the sort of task monuments are called on to perform? Perhaps. This monument, such as it is, is being called upon to enable a sort of remembrance. Not unlike other monuments, this monument would be responsible to history as a reminder for us. And even if this makes sense, monuments are conventionally charged to call into remembrance something for which *we* wish to be remembered: "[a] work intended to celebrate and preserve the memory of a person, an event, or an idea"[27]—great battles, great historical figures, moments in time, points in space.

One might say that a monument *to* something is an anchor of presence dropped into time by a people unsure that they will be remembered. Monuments are left to posterity to things worth remembering, to things of value, that we value, things for which we wish to be remembered. In this sense such undertakings are not about the future. Rather, they are about the anxiety of the present—an ontological anxiety—with respect to the very uncertainty of the future. It is a desire to make permanent that which threatens to disappear irretrievably. The very idea of a monument to something we wish would never have come to presence to begin with is exceedingly odd.

I do not mean to say that monuments are always explicitly affirmative. There is, of course, also a deep affinity between monument and atrocity, between monument and disaster suffered upon memory. And indeed the late-twentieth-century countermonument may be read as having as its principal concern the very anxiety of its own assertion as a monument.[28] No longer is the public space of the monument an unproblematic site of memory, a prophylactic against forgetting, and compensation for the symbolic debt of the past. Rather, the countermonument seeks only the afterimage of its effect, the memory, the remainder of the monument's assertion. As a political praxis and an ethical injunction, the contemporary ethico-political shift in the practice of the monument is a troubling development for the modern monument in the desert. Monuments that disappear, that inhabit the negative space of their shadows, that are assertions of an absence—these features simply add to the ambiguity of the desert project. The commemorative responsibility of the modern monument (regardless of what it is or how well this responsibility may be met) is to stand for events. It is the monument—not the community and not memory—that is the bearer of the responsibility, and this is precisely what countermonumental strategies seek to challenge.

It is important to recognize that the commemorative work of such monuments—even if the injunction "do not forget" remains the same—is always a function of the particular needs (political or otherwise) of a given community. One can see this in the way holocaust memory is commemorated in remarkably different forms according to the location and time in which it is carried out, the political climate in which it is constructed, and the specific character of the rupture with the past it attempts to bridge.[29]

The way in which monuments mean, or refer, is clearly never straightforward. The didactic, symbolic, and functional dimensions of the monument must always come into conflict with other countervailing forces: denial, forgetting, disavowal, and resistance. This is not to say that some monuments do not favor certain forms of historical memory over others (official versus community sites, community versus individual mourning), but there remains a necessarily participatorial dimension of the monument as site. The place where the monument and witness intersect constitutes an event; it is here that one may locate the production of meaning.

It is precisely in this sense that a monument to waste is an inversion of its work as a monument. To the extent that it draws our attention, it does so not entirely to the past nor exactly to the future. It has the task of perpetuating a memory, but the memory must be of itself. It exalts nothing. It must assert its real danger, but it must do so in an idiom if not entirely foreign to such messages, then at least one to which it is very ambiguously related. Its concern is the perpetual present, the now in which the witness must not fail to understand.

The official position on the desert monument acknowledges the difficulty of the projection of meaning, the fragility of memory, and the unprecedented temporal duration of concern. The recourse to a system of monuments to deal with these problems was deemed more or less obvious. Some thought was given to the persistence and intelligibility of various manmade monuments (e.g., the pyramids of Giza, 2600–2500 B.C.; Stonehenge, 2700–2500 B.C. Nazca Lines of Peru, 200 B.C.–A.D. 600; Serpent Mound of Ohio, 1000 B.C.–A.D. 700; the Acropolis, 447–424 B.C.). And some thought was given to the temporal dimensions of communicative acts, the structure of future societies, and the shifting landscape of language. The problem, however, remains that the monument, wedded to its site (as though it were a ruin), is not envisioned as equally wedded to any memory. In this sense the monument is seen as archival. The site will disgorge its meaning to its witness merely in the form of a warning with respect to the site itself. In this way the monument's concern in its gesture toward itself is that it convey a mimetic performance of the danger of the waste, the length of time it has been interred, and some manner of a do-not-open-before date. That is, a message, not a memory.

SIGN

The figure of the monument has been grasped in a very interesting manner by those charged to think about it. They have understood the monument as something that conveys meaning. *Some things just mean what they mean.* Which is, of course, very different from saying that things simply signify before we know *what* they signify, that the signified is given without being known. Deleuze and Guattari illustrate this point: "Your wife looked at you with a funny expression. And this morning the mailman handed you a letter from the IRS and crossed his fingers. Then you stepped in a pile of dog shit. . . . It doesn't matter what it means, it's still signifying."[30] That is, the monument's designers began with the assumption that certain physical forms have the capacity to convey extralinguistic, stable pancultural meaning. Furthermore, they asserted that this capacity is based on an "enduring human propensity to experience common and stable meanings in the physical form of things, including the design of landscapes and built-places."[31] To illustrate this claim they would point, for example, to the "powerful feelings invoked" in the viewer in the presence of the paintings at Lascaux or Altamira.

There is an assumption of a capacity on the side of the object (to be a vehicle of transmission) and a propensity on the side of the human (to perceive and experience objects similarly). The result is the notion of archetype, a fortuitous notion since it seems to offer a way to avoid the problem of temporal semiotic decay. The work of ethologist Iranäus Eibl-Eibesfeldt moved smoothly into this structure of universal meaning. He used faces (seen in Figure 8.3) expressing horror, revulsion, fear, pain, and anguish—providing support for an essential, phenomenological, or haptic mode of perception.

The image on the left in Figure 8.3 (clearly borrowed from Edvard Munch's painting "The Scream"), together with the image on the right from Eibl-Eibesfeldt ("which conveys disgust, as for something nauseating or poisonous"), as human faces framing a message (DANGER . . .), the monument's designers felt,

DANGER
POISONOUS RADIOACTIVE ☢ WASTE BURIED HERE
DO NOT DIG OR DRILL HERE BEFORE 12,000 A.D.

8.3 Danger. From Trauth, Hora, and Guzowski (see caption 8.1), F-114.

would "indicate that the message is a warning and invite its decipherment as a precaution to any intrusion on the site."[32]

THREAT

An ecological or nuclear threat cannot be understood as a simple threat—a promise or a debt and accountable in terms of risk and reparation. It is more complex, diffuse than this and as such presents a problem that exceeds traditional (or at least conventional) modes of conceptualization. The ecological threat comes to pose a problem of the real.

The real, specifically the Lacanian Real, is an event that always arrives unannounced—no threat, no warning. The ethical reflection that Lacan has said lies at the core of analytic practice is called to an encounter only afterward, once it is too late. It is the debt as effect that arrives first, making the call to ethical reflection "too late"—the real is traumatic, and the repetition that ensues negates the possibility of paying the debt now owed; the wound, that is, opened by the intrusion of the real. The pathologies of response, bound to the machinery of the imaginary/pleasure principle, are ceaselessly invoked to cover over the wound of the real, but the wound persists.

But is it the retroactive discovery of the real's irruption into life that is the ethical call, or can it be viewed otherwise? Clearly, it is the "too" that is singularly important here. Is the call heard "too" late? It may be too late for some things. The Alliance of Small Island States made exactly this claim in Kyoto. It will be too late for us, they said; the water's rising—meaning it was already too late. It was too late for Chernobyl when the foreseeable arrived unexpectedly. But it's too late as well for those things that have not entered public consciousness or those that once had but have since slipped away. The wall of mud and rock and debris that smashed into the Vargas area north of Caracas, Venezuela (December 1999), displacing the already displaced, flashed up only briefly as a concern. But when the Payatas dump outside Metro Manila (home to a third of Manila's daily domestic waste—approximately 4 million households—and, as a result, for around 20,000 scavengers) collapsed in June 2000, the thousand-plus who were buried alive hardly registered. The accident, though, stands apart from this. It collapses the too soon and the too late, leaving us, in its early (and thus anticipated) arrival, too late to respond, even as we do so.

After Slavoj Zizek, we can say there are three typical responses to the real of ecological crisis.[33] The predominant reaction belongs to those who resist the very idea of a crisis. Nothing to worry about, after all. This operates within the register of disavowal (*Verleugnung*)—I know it's true, but all the same . . . For those who respond to the threat of ecological crisis outside the register of disavowal, there are two typical modes: there are those who respond with obsessive (neurotic) activity and those who elect to read into the crisis a message (psychotic) issuing from the real. In the first instance, the threat elicits an obsessional economy such that frenzied activity must be maintained so the calamitous event *x* does not take place. Much like Julia Kristeva's description of the obsessional as valuing the procedural over the declarative, the obsessional in this case associates each situation with a requirement to do something—if x, then *do* y (not x *means* y). A "paradoxical doing," writes Kristeva, "acts (−1)." This is a kind of doing that is deprived of its logical relation to an affect, where the signifier is dissociated from the "psychic representative of affect."[34] And quite simply, the result is a compulsion to search for other semiotic means of (displaced) expression—gestural, visual, mobile.

In the second case—which also resonates somewhat with the "nature bats last" school of environmentalism[35]—threats and crises are taken to be very specific kinds of signs. As a set of signs, the ecological crisis is presumed to be indexically related to a normatively charged (and generally pissed-off) nature. The crises—global warming, ozone depletion, overpopulation, nuclear weapons, water pollution and shortage, the Soviet nuclear industry, postindustrial Eastern Europe, smog, and AIDS all come to mind—are read symptomatically as providing a link between a manifest crisis and a disrupted or transgressed nature. These crises tell a story—or they at least sketch out the implications of a larger narrative—concerning the ecological, and therefore moral, improprieties of "Man."

These three responses can be understood as pathologies (and therefore strategies) directed at avoiding an encounter with the real of ecological threats.[36] The pathologies of response are united on the level that they are directed at blinding one to the fact of the "irreducible gap separating the real from the modes of its symbolization."[37]

THE REAL

Chernobyl illustrates well the liminal characteristics of the real's irruption into reality. The Russian filmmaker Vladimir Shevchenko headed the first film crew

8.4 Black Hole. Concept by Michael Brill; art by Safdar Abidi.

permitted into the "red zone" (a 30-square-kilometer area that was emptied of 100,000 residents in the days and weeks following the accident). The short, part-black-and-white, part-color documentary that resulted, *Chernobyl: Chronicle of Difficult Weeks,* is in one sense simply a clumsy piece of propaganda meant to show how well the Soviet scientific, technical, and military and Communist Party authorities came together in the face of great adversity to overcome the severity of the accident. We see footage of numerous meetings, party officials extolling the virtues of cooperation and hard work, and evacuees warmly embracing their hosts in their new communities.[38]

But what was extraordinary about this film was a sequence in which the film crew was aboard a helicopter circling, not very high, above the smoldering remains of the reactor building. The voice-over, dubbed in English, was saying something about "black and white, the color of disaster." But what we see on the surface of the film are millions of tiny pops and scratches. The filmmakers explain that they had initially assumed they had inadvertently used defective film stock. It was only later that they discovered that the problem with the film had nothing to do with the film itself. The surface distortions were in fact caused by decay particles that came into contact with the film while inside the camera. The irradiated film had captured a trace of the real, a pointillism of the real—discovered only retroactively. There is simply no correspondence of the film and its heroic worker narrative spin with the brute irruption of the real that is captured, incidentally, as the paradoxical urtext of the film: "The paradox of the Lacanian Real, then, is that it is an entity which, although it does not exist (in the sense of [. . .] taking place in reality), has a series of properties—it exercises a certain structural causality, it can produce a series of effects in the symbolic reality of subjects."[39]

Yet it is not as though the real is only a raw material from which, and upon which, the symbolic makes a world. This may be so for the neonate (the confused, solipsistic empiricist, as the Montreal psychoanalyst Charles Levin quipped), but it is the "real after the letter"—the real that shows up in language as paradox and aporia—that is of interest here.[40] The thing with the real is that it is both presupposed and posed by the symbolic.[41] It is only discovered by the distortions it produces in the symbolic world, but, in turn, the symbolic can only function by circulating through these zones of distortion—places where symbolization falters. The real "resists symbolization absolutely."[42] The real of the ecological crisis can only be inferred retroactively through its repercussions within the symbolic. And these repercussions are felt only as holes, or gaps, in the symbolic itself.

MEMORY

I, for one, would like to stand as the little human drawings in front of something intended and required to last longer than anything built in Alexander's time or before. I would like to participate in this project of aesthetic longing for the intensity of the extreme. But the question remains, what practices might be equal to the intent of such a site?

The monument must always work this way: either forgetting to remember or remembering to forget. It must only allow the past to be present in the form of a threat to life. The penitence cannot fully consign the threat to a past, to any past. This is the problem: fear. And trembling. Jacques Derrida writes: "We tremble in that strange repetition that ties an irrefutable past (a shock has been felt, a traumatism has already affected us) to a future that cannot be anticipated. . . . I tremble at what exceeds my seeing and my knowing . . . a secret always makes you tremble."[43] The auguries are not very favorable. Both, that is, in the present sense—that of a future—and in the sense that the monument (a monument) is to carry the burden of memory of that which cannot be recalled: the recollection of the unrecallable in the face of the incomprehensible.

A material trace, the visibility of the monument, supported not by a collective and encompassing memory but by an archival assemblage. In the desert: you are here.

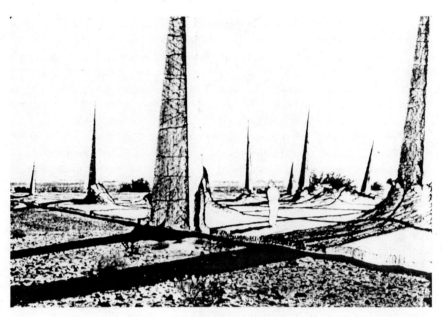

8.5 Spikes bursting through grid. Concept by Michael Brill; art by Safdar Abidi.

NOTES

1. The subject matter of this text belongs to a larger work, forthcoming in 2004 from the University of Minnesota Press under the title *Signs of Danger: An Essay on Waste, Threat, and Trauma.*

2. This is key, and it is in part what marks contemporary techno-scientific endeavors as unique. See Paul Virilio, "The Museum of Accidents," *Public* 2 (1989): 81–85; Paul Virilio, "The Primal Accident," in *The Politics of Everyday Fear,* ed. and trans. Brian Massumi (Minneapolis: University of Minnesota Press, 1993).

3. See Søren Kierkegaard, *The Concept of Anxiety: A Simple Psychologically Orienting Deliberation on the Dogmatic Issue of Hereditary Sin* (Princeton: Princeton University Press, 1980): "If I am anxious about a past misfortune, then this is not because it is in the past but because it may be repeated, i.e., become future"; 91.

4. Gilles Deleuze and Félix Guattari, *A Thousand Plateaus,* trans. Brian Massumi (Minneapolis: University of Minnesota Press, 1987), 288, italics added.

5. Ibid.

6. Ibid.

7. Jean Baudrillard, *Cool Memories II,* trans. Chris Turner (Durham, NC: Duke University Press, 1996), 14–15.

8. Ibid. This is not, however, to align Baudrillard with Deleuze and Guattari with respect to the secret. Elsewhere—particularly Jean Baudrillard, *Seduction,* trans. Brian Singer (Montreal: New World Perspectives, 1990)—he makes it clear that the

secret is a kind of pact in which the content of the secret is secondary or even incidental to the keeping of it; that is, to its remaining unspoken (see 79–81).

9. One of the Stealth's most recent public disclosures was in the form of decidedly visible images of wreckage broadcast on Serbian television in 1999.

10. I am recklessly paraphrasing from Derrida's thoughts on secrecy in "*Tout autre est tout autre,*" in Jacques Derrida, *The Gift of Death,* trans. David Wills (Chicago: University of Chicago Press, 1995), 82–115.

11. It is unclear to me whether the null hypothesis was really an idea or an alibi. After all, it would cost a fraction of the proposed amount to bury the waste in an unmarked site—providing a compelling incentive for the project to be spun in this direction. But on the other hand, doing so would make invisible the very gesture of interment.

12. U.S. Environmental Protection Agency, "Environmental Standards for the Management and Disposal of Spent Nuclear Fuel, High-Level and Transuranic Radioactive Wastes: Final Rule, 40 CFR Part 191," *Federal Register* 50, 182 (1985): 38066–38089.

13. Quoted in Kathleen M. Trauth, Stephen C. Hora, and Robert V. Guzowski, *Expert Judgment on Markers to Deter Inadvertent Human Intrusion Into the Waste Isolation Pilot Plant* (Albuquerque, NM: Sandia National Laboratories, 1983).

14. Human Interference Task Force, *Reducing the Likelihood of Future Human Activities That Could Affect Geologic High-Level Waste Repositories* (Columbus, OH: Office of Nuclear Waste Isolation, Battelle Memorial Institute, 1984).

15. Thomas A. Sebeok, *Communication Measures to Bridge Ten Millennia* (Columbus, OH: Office of Nuclear Waste Isolation, Battelle Memorial Institute, 1984), 24.

16. Ibid.

17. Ibid., 27.

18. Ibid, italics added.

19. A. Weitzberg, *Building on Existing Institutions to Perpetuate Knowledge of Waste Repositories* (Columbus, OH: Office of Nuclear Waste Isolation, Battelle Memorial Institute, 1982).

20. Percy H. Tannenbaum, *Communication Across 300 Generations: Deterring Human Interference With Waste Disposal Sites* (Columbus, OH: Office of Nuclear Waste Isolation, Battelle Memorial Institute, 1984).

21. Cf. Irenäus Eibl-Eibesfeldt, *Human Ethology* (New York: Aldine de Gruyter, 1989).

22. See Maureen Kaplan, *Archaeological Data as a Basis for Repository Marker Design,* ed. Analytical Sciences Corporation (Columbus, OH: Office of Nuclear Waste Isolation, Battelle Memorial Institute, 1982); Maureen Kaplan and Mel Adams, "Using the Past to Protect the Future: Marking Nuclear Waste Disposal Sites," *Archaeology* 39 (September-October 1986): 51–54. Aspects of Kaplan's work built on previous work of Givens. See D. B. Givens, "From Here to Eternity: Communicating With the Distant Future," *Et Cetera: A Review of General Semantics* 39, 2 (1982): 159–179.

23. Trauth, Hora, and Guzowski, *Expert Judgment*.

24. I develop this point at length elsewhere, but the question of the center—of whether there ought to be a center of the site—figured prominently in design discussions. It is, I think, an important question—at least insofar as how the idea of a center relates to such an undertaking—but one that was handled in a rather puzzling fashion. On the one hand, there is a stated intention to invert the "traditional symbolic meaning of the center" as the assertion of presence—"as the act marking order (Cosmos) out of undifferentiation (Chaos)" (ibid., F52). Yet on the other hand, in a discussion of maps to be included on the site, the designers advocate (in addition to a world map of waste sites) a diagram showing the longitude and latitude of global waste sites *relative to* the WIPP (ibid., F114) The proposed system of representation would allow the WIPP to usurp Greenwich and the Equator to become 0.0, the center par excellence.

25. Cathy Caruth, *Unclaimed Experience: Trauma, Narrative, and History* (Baltimore: John Hopkins University Press, 1991).

26. Toronto filmmaker and director Peter Blow's remarkable documentary, *Village of Widows,* tracks an instance of escape. This extremely powerful short film follows an ethical line of implication/flight from the Dene of Great Slave Lake, through Port Hope, Ontario, the Manhattan Project, to Hiroshima. The Great Slave Dene continue to endure the loss of nearly a generation of their men to radiation-related sickness—attributable to their employment (in the 1940s) mining and transporting uranium. This uranium was refined in Port Hope, then transported to the United States where it was made into the bombs (the Manhattan Project) detonated over Japan. In the wake of their history of traumatic loss and within their ongoing suffering, the Dene reached the conclusion that they, too, were complicit in the bombing. Their ethical obligation was to make an extraordinary visit to Hiroshima to tell the Japanese survivors they were sorry, that they didn't know, and that they, too, would commemorate the stunning loss of life. For an exploration of the problematics of this history, see my "Highway of the Atom: Recollections Along a Route," *Topia: A Canadian Journal of Cultural Studies* 7 (2002): 99–115.

27. Harold Osborne, *The Oxford Companion to Art* (London: Oxford University Press, 1970), 737.

28. Here I think of the Gerzes' disappearing "Harburg Monument Against Fascism," detailed in James E. Young, "The Counter-Monument: Memory Against Itself in Germany Today," *Critical Inquiry* 18, 2 (1992): 267–296.

29. Cf. Andreas Huyssen, "Monument and Memory in a Postmodern Age," in *The Art of Memory: Holocaust Memorials in History,* ed. James E. Young (Munich: Prestel-Verlag, 1994), 13–14.

30. Deleuze and Guattari, *A Thousand Plateaus,* 112.

31. Trauth, Hora, and Guzowski, *Expert Judgment,* F39.

32. Ibid., F114. See also Irenäus Eibl-Eibesfeldt, *Human Ethology* (New York: Aldine de Gruyter, 1989); Irenäus Eibl-Eibesfeldt, *Ethology: The Biology of Human Behavior,* trans. Erich Klinghammer (New York: Holt, Rinehart, and Winston, 1975).

33. See Slavoj Zizek, *Looking Awry: An Introduction to Jacques Lacan Through Popular Culture* (Cambridge: MIT Press, 1991), 34–39.

34. Julia Kristeva, *New Maladies of the Soul,* trans. Ross Guberman (New York: Columbia University Press, 1995), 44–49.

35. I explore this theme in *Primitives in the Wilderness: Deep Ecology and the Missing Human Subject* (Albany: State University of New York Press, 1997).

36. For Freud there was a kinship between disavowal and psychosis that does not exist (in the same fashion) with neurosis. The very movement of disavowal is what founds psychosis and what effectively creates an opposition between psychosis and neurosis. In both cases, as Freud described it (1924), there is a loss of reality, a rebellion of the id against the world. Also in both cases it is in relation to the id that a negotiation takes place—a preponderance of reality over id in the case of neurosis and the reverse in psychosis. "In neurosis a part of reality is avoided by a sort of flight, but in psychosis it [reality] is remodeled." Sigmund Freud, "The Loss of Reality in Neurosis and Psychosis (1924)," trans. Joan Riviere, in *Collected Papers, Volume 5* (New York: Basic, 1959), 279. Which is to say that in the neurotic response to the ecological threat, there is no attempt to disavow a reality but merely to ignore it through a repression. Whereas on the other hand, the psychotic response is to disavow it entirely and put something else in its place, to refashion a reality through the active construction of perception and falsification of memory (that is, "by creating a new reality which is no longer open to objections like that which has been forsaken"; ibid., 279).

37. Zizek, *Looking Awry,* 36.

38. Vladimir Shevchenko, *Chernobyl: Chronicle of Difficult Weeks* (Oakland: The Video Project, 16mm b&w and color, trans. to video, 54 min., 1986).

39. Slavoj Zizek, *The Sublime Object of Ideology* (London: Verso, 1989), 163.

40. See Bruce Fink, *The Lacanian Subject: Between Language and Jouissance* (Princeton: Princeton University Press, 1995), 24–29. The postulate of "two different levels of the real: (1) a real before the letter, that is a presymbolic real, which, in the final analysis [so to speak], is but our own hypothesis (R_1), and (2) a real after the letter, which is characterized by impasses and impossibilities due to the relations among the elements of the symbolic order itself (R_2), that is, which is generated by the symbolic"; 27.

41. Zizek, *Sublime Object of Ideology,* 131–133.

42. Jacques Lacan, *The Seminar of Jacques Lacan: Book I: Freud's Papers on Technique 1953–1954,* trans. John Forrester (New York: W. W. Norton, 1988), 66.

43. Jacques Derrida, *The Gift of Death,* trans. David Wills (Chicago: University of Chicago Press, 1995), 53–54.

Contributors

Michael A. Amundson is associate professor of history at Northern Arizona University. His publications include *Yellowcake Towns: Uranium Mining Communities in the American West* (Boulder: University Press of Colorado, 2002) and two articles on uranium mining, "Mining the Grand Canyon to Save It: The Orphan Lode Uranium Mine and National Security," *Western Historical Quarterly* 32 (Autumn 2001), and "Home on the Range No More: The Boom and Bust of a Wyoming Uranium Mining Town," *Western Historical Quarterly* 25 (Winter 1995). He also contributed a chapter, "Yellowcake to Singletrack: Class, Culture, and Identity in Moab, Utah," on the town's transition from uranium mining boomtown to mountain biking boomtown in Liza Nichols et al., eds., *Imagining the Big Open: Nature, Identity and Play in the New West* (Salt Lake City: University of Utah Press, 2003).

Mick Broderick is associate director of the Centre for Millennial Studies (Australian branch) and lectures in media analysis at Murdoch University in Perth, Western Australia. He has been writing on cultural aspects of nuclear energy for nearly twenty years. His books include *Nuclear Movies* (Jefferson, NC: McFarland, 1991) and *Hibakusha Cinema* (London: Kegan Paul, 1996;

Tokyo: Gendai Shokan, 1999), and he has written for numerous journals and collections.

Peter Goin is professor of photography and videography at the University of Nevada, Reno. His publications include *Nuclear Landscapes* (Baltimore: Johns Hopkins University Press, 1991) and several photo essays on America's atomic landscape. Goin's other publications include *Tracing the Line: A Photographic Survey of the Mexican-American Border* (Reno: Library, University of Nevada, Reno, 1987), *Arid Waters: Photographs From the Water in the West Project,* with Ellen Manchester (Reno: University of Nevada Press, 1992), *Humanature* (University of Texas Press, 1996), *Changing Mines in America,* coauthored with C. Elizabeth Raymond (Harrisonburg, VA: Center for American Places, 2003), and *A Doubtful River,* with Robert Dawson and Mary Webb (Reno: University of Nevada Press, 2000). Goin is also a coauthor of *Atlas of the New West* (New York: Norton, 1997).

Jon Hunner is professor of history at New Mexico State University. He is author of *Inventing Los Alamos: The Creation of an Atomic Culture, 1943–1957,* forthcoming from the University of Oklahoma Press. He also coauthored *Santa Fe: A Historic Walking Tour* (Chicago: Arcadia, 2000), which uses historic photographs to tell the history of the "City Different." He contributed a chapter on how World War II changed the West in Richard Etulain's *Peopling the American West* (Albuquerque: University of New Mexico Press, forthcoming). In addition to teaching U.S. history, Hunner also directs the Public History Program at NMSU.

Ferenc M. Szasz is Regent's professor of history at the University of New Mexico. He has published several articles on atomic history and is the author of *The Day the Sun Rose Twice* (Albuquerque: University of New Mexico Press, 1984). Szasz's other books include *British Scientists and the Manhattan Project: The Los Alamos Years* (New York: St. Martin's, 1992), *The Protestant Clergy in the Great Plains and Mountain West, 1865–1915* (Albuquerque: University of New Mexico Press, 1988), *The Divided Mind of Protestant America, 1880–1930* (University: University of Alabama Press, 1982), and *Scots in the North American West, 1790–1917* (Norman: University of Oklahoma Press, 2000).

A. Costandina Titus is professor of political science at the University of Nevada, Las Vegas, and a Nevada state senator. Her publications on atomic topics include *Bombs in the Backyard: Atomic Testing and American Culture,* 2nd ed. (Reno:

University of Nevada Press, 2001), "From 'Atomic Bomb Baby' to 'Nuclear Funeral': Atomic Music Comes of Age, 1945–1990," *Popular Music and Society* (Winter 1990), "Selling the Bomb: The Government and Hollywood Join Forces at Ground Zero," *Halcyon: A Journal of the Humanities* (1984), "Governmental Responsibility for Victims of Atomic Testing: A Chronicle of the Politics of Compensation," *Journal of Health Politics, Policy, and Law* (Summer 1983), and "Back to Ground Zero: Old Footage Through New Lenses," *Journal of Popular Film and Television* (Spring 1983). Titus is also a board member of the Nevada Test Site Historical Foundation.

Peter C. van Wyck is assistant professor of communication studies at Concordia University. His publications include *Primitives in the Wilderness: Deep Ecology and the Missing Human Subject* (Albany: State University of New York Press, 1997) and the forthcoming book, *Signs of Danger: An Essay on Waste, Threat, and Trauma* (Minneapolis: University of Minnesota Press).

Scott C. Zeman is associate professor of history at New Mexico Tech. His publications include *Chronology of the American West* (Santa Barbara: ABC-CLIO, 2002), "Monument Valley: Shaping the Image of the Southwest's Cultural Cross-roads," *Journal of Arizona History* (Autumn 1998), "Historian Louis M. Hacker's 'Coincidental Conversion' to the Truth," *Historian* (Fall 1998), and " 'The Truth of a Mad Man': Collective Memory and Representation of the Holocaust in the Partisans of Vilna (1986) and the Documentary Genre," *Film and History* 32, 1 (2002).

Index